CAMBRIDGE
UNIVERSITY PRESS

ICT Starters

On Track Stage 1

Victoria Ellis, Sarah Lawrey and Doug Dickinson

CAMBRIDGE
UNIVERSITY PRESS

University Printing House, Cambridge CB2 8BS, United Kingdom

One Liberty Plaza, 20th Floor, New York, NY 10006, USA

477 Williamstown Road, Port Melbourne, VIC 3207, Australia

314–321, 3rd Floor, Plot 3, Splendor Forum, Jasola District Centre, New Delhi – 110025, India

79 Anson Road, #06–04/06, Singapore 079906

Cambridge University Press is part of the University of Cambridge.

It furthers the University's mission by disseminating knowledge in the pursuit of education, learning and research at the highest international levels of excellence.

www.cambridge.org
Information on this title: www.cambridge.org/9781108463546

© Cambridge University Press 2019

First published 2003
Second edition 2005
Third edition 2013
Fourth edition 2019

20 19 18 17 16 15 14 13 12 11 10 9 8 7 6 5 4 3 2 1

Printed in the United Kingdom by Latimer Trend

A catalogue record for this publication is available from the British Library

ISBN 978-1-108-46354-6 Paperback

Additional resources for this publication at www.cambridge.org/9781108463546

Cambridge University Press has no responsibility for the persistence or accuracy of URLs for external or third-party internet websites referred to in this publication, and does not guarantee that any content on such websites is, or will remain, accurate or appropriate. Information regarding prices, travel timetables, and other factual information given in this work is correct at the time of first printing but Cambridge University Press does not guarantee the accuracy of such information thereafter.

All exam-style questions and sample answers in this title were written by the authors. In examinations, the way marks are awarded may be different.

....

Introduction

Cambridge ICT Starters: On Track Stage 1 has been written to support you in your work for the Cambridge International Diploma ICT Starters syllabus (On Track Stage 1) from 2019. This book provides full coverage of all of the modules so that you will have a good platform of skills and information to support you in the next stages of your development of ICT capability. The modules can be studied in any order and helps you to strengthen your key skills and knowledge of basic routines required at this level to become more competent at handling data, basic spreadsheet management, as well as creating and editing written work and handling images.

The book will provide you and your helpers with:

- examples of activities to complete
- exercises to practise the skills before you put them into practice
- final projects to reflect on just how much you have learnt
- optional extension and challenge activities for those who want to challenge themselves further.

The book has been designed for use in the classroom, with help and support from trained teachers. The tasks, skills and activities have been set in real-life situations, where computer access will be essential. At the beginning of each module, there is a section called 'Before you start …' which explains the things you need to know before you begin your work. The activities are designed to guide you towards a final project, where you will have the opportunity to demonstrate your knowledge and understanding of each of the skills.

Some exercises require you to access pre-prepared files for editing. These files are available to your teachers from www.cambridge.org/9781108463546. These files are included to help you start the activities in this book.

The modules in this book refer to examples from Microsoft Office 2016, and Microsoft Access. Using these applications will help you develop your digital skills and will mean that the notes and activities in the book should be easy for you to follow. However, your teacher might decide to use different applications to help you to meet the module objectives.

We hope that you will enjoy working on this stage and take pleasure in developing your ICT skills!

Good luck!

Contents

How to use this book

In every module, look out for these features:

Module objectives: This table shows you the key things that you will learn in this module.

	In this module, you will learn how to:	Pass/Merit	Done?
1	Create a plan for a presentation	P	
2	Recognise and select appropriate source materials	P	

Key terms: These boxes provide with you definitions of words that may be important or useful.

> **Key term**
>
> **Text style:** this is how text will look. It includes the font style, size and colour.

Did you know?: These boxes provide interesting information and opportunities for further research.

> **Did you know?**
>
> More than 30 million presentations are created each day using Microsoft PowerPoint.

Tip: These boxes give you handy hints as you work.

> **Tip**
>
> Greater than 100 is written as >100.

Challenge: These activities are more difficult and extend beyond the syllabus.

Challenge

Scenario: These are tasks that help you practise everything you have learnt in the module in a "real-life" situation.

Scenario

School library

Pass/Merit: This shows you the level of all of the activities in the book.

Skill box: These boxes contain activities for you to test what you have learnt.

Skill 1

Watch out!: These boxes help you to avoid making mistakes in your work.

> **WATCH OUT!**
>
> Be careful when using the 'Replace All' option as you might end up replacing parts of words rather than whole words.

Stay safe!: These boxes contain important e-safety advice.

> **Stay safe!**
>
> When using the internet for research, make sure that you only use trusted websites.

	In this module, you will learn how to:	Pass/Merit	Done?
1	Create and format text that is suitable for a particular purpose	P	
2	Adjust properties to allow graphics, or other objects, to fit correctly within the document	P	
3	Insert a table into a document	P	
4	Use advanced formatting features	M	
5	Use page-formatting options	M	
6	Adjust page formatting for a specific audience.	M	

Did you know?

Microsoft Word used to have a little assistant called Clippy to help you on-screen. Clippy looked like a paperclip. Some people loved Clippy but others felt he was an irritation. Clippy was retired along with the 2007 version of Word.

In this module, you are going to develop your skills in creating documents for a purpose, that will help you work towards your final project. The aim of the project will be to improve the layout of your school's guide to the internet. The guide will be used at one of the school's internet events, so it will need to be well presented!

To enable you to do this, you are going to need to use some advanced formatting techniques to create clear and well-designed documents. You will learn to format both the text and the page itself, to make the document more appealing to your audience. This will include inserting tables and bullet points into a document.

You will also learn about:

- how to use the find and replace tool
- how to add hyperlinks to a document
- how to add a cover page to a document.

Before you start

You should know how to:

- type text into a document
- insert images into a document
- format text in a document, including the font style, size and colour
- underline text or change it to bold or italics.

Introduction

It is an important and extremely useful skill to be able to create a formal-looking document. It takes a lot of experience and hard work to learn how to successfully create effective types of **text styles**, how to place images in suitable locations and how to use white space effectively. If you can create a formal-looking document, you can create a great impression on your teachers and even future employers that will have a lasting impact. It will show anybody reading your document that care and attention has gone into the making of it. It is likely that you will need to experiment with different text styles and placement of images, to find the best style and layout for the content in your document. The type of style and layout that you choose will often depend on the audience accessing it, as well as the intended purpose of your document.

> **Key term**
>
> **Text style:** this is how text will look. It includes the font style, size and colour.

Skill 1

Setting and using text styles

When you create a document, you might find that you are setting the same text **formatting** options repeatedly. For example, whenever you type a new title, you might need to change the font size, font style and font colour to the specific settings that you have chosen for your title.

It is really useful to create a text style that applies all these settings at once. People usually create a text style for their title and the main body of their text. However, you could create many different styles for different purposes, including subheadings and sections of text that you want to emphasise.

> **Key term**
>
> **Formatting:** changing the style of text and images.

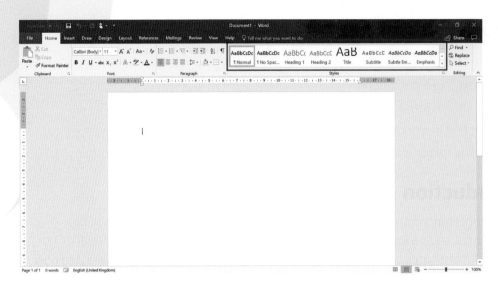

Key terms

Tab: an area in the software that contains settings.

Window: a viewing area that opens when you click a button. It can be used to display different options on your screen.

To create a new text style you should:

1. Click on the **Home tab** and click on the arrow at the end of the 'Styles' section.

2. Click on the option 'Create a Style'. This will open a **window** that will allow you to name the style that you want to create.

3. Type a name for your text style in the 'Name' box.

4. Choose a suitable name that will allow you easily to recognise the style and its purpose within your document. For example, you could name a style: 'My_Title' so that it can be easily found and applied whenever you create a new title for your document. When you have typed in a name for your text style, click on 'Modify'.

This will now open a window that you can use to format the text.

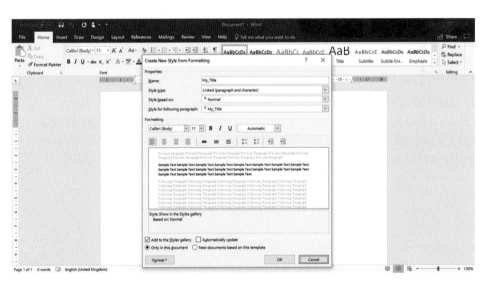

Tip

If a text style already exists with the name that you have chosen, a window will appear telling you this. You will need to choose another suitable name.

5. You do not need to change any of the settings in the 'Properties' section. Under the 'Formatting' section, you will be able to set the font style, font size, whether it is in bold, italic or underlined, as well as the font colour.

6. When you have selected the font setting that you wish to use, click on 'OK'.

7   You should now see your text style within the text styles section under the **Home** tab.

8   To apply your text style to any text, highlight the section of text that you want to format and click on the text style that you have created.

Activity 1.1

Open the document 'Newsletter.docx' that your teacher has provided you with. Create a text style called 'My_Title'. Set the text style to font style 'Verdana', font size 18 and font colour blue. Then, apply the text style to your title 'School Newsletter'.

Activity 1.2

Create a text style called 'My_Subheading'. Set the text font style to 'Bookman Old Style' and set as font size 14. Next, change the text to bold and change the font colour to dark blue. Then, apply the text style to the two subheadings 'Recent News' and 'Forthcoming Events'.

Activity 1.3

Create a text style called 'Picture_Caption'. Set the text font style to 'Bookman Old Style', font size 10, italics and font colour black. Apply the text style to the caption text underneath the image.

Activity 1.4

Create a text style called 'Body_text'. Set the text font style to 'Bookman Old Style', font size 12 and font colour black. Then apply the text style to the remaining text in the document.

Finally, save your document using the filename 'My_Newsletter.docx'.

Skill 2

Using text wrapping

Sometimes, you will need to include both text and images in a document. When this happens, you will need to make use of the space you have on the page to make sure that your design looks good. The way that you place an image alongside the text within a document, can have a very positive effect on the design.

You might want to wrap the text around the image, to make best use of the space available. This will ensure that there are no large sections of empty white space being left on the page. When you add the **text wrapping** setting, the effect will be added to the image and not to the text. This means that the text will wrap around the image, using the setting you have selected. This can be done in several different ways, outlined below.

Key term

Text wrapping: when text is set to follow the outline of an image.

To set text wrapping for an image, you should:

1 insert an image into your document.

2 select the image.

3 click on the **Format** tab and the **Wrap Text** button.

A menu will now appear with all the text wrapping options for you to choose from.

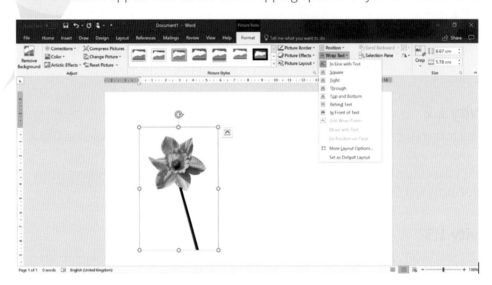

This is what the options do:

- The 'Square' option means that a box will be placed around the image and the text will be wrapped around the box. This box is called a 'bounding box'.

- The 'Tight' option means that an outline is placed around the image and the text is wrapped to follow the outline. If the image is square or rectangle in shape, it will not look any different from the square wrap when it is used.

- The 'Through' option allows text to flow into any white space available within an image. When you first apply the through option, it won't look any different from the square or tight option. To make the text flow into the white space, you will need to use the settings to edit the wrap points.

- The 'Top and Bottom' option means text will wrap around the top and bottom of the image but not the sides.

- The 'Behind Text' option means that the image is placed behind any text, so the text will be seen over the top of the image.

- The 'In Front of Text' option means that the image is placed in front of any text, so the text will be behind the image.

- The 'Edit Wrap Points' option allows you to change the specific points where the text wraps around the image. This option is also available within the text wrapping menu. This is most useful when the text wrapping options are set at 'Tight' and 'Through'. It also means that you can bring the text closer to, or move the text further away from, certain parts of the image.

- To edit a wrap point, apply the text wrapping style to the image and then click the menu option 'Edit Wrap Points'.

- A red outline will now appear around the image with little black squares, indicating the wrap points. If you move any of the little black squares, you will see the text wrapping for the image change in appearance. You can also add additional wrap points by clicking on the red line and dragging it. You should be able to see an extra black square when you do this.

When you have applied the text wrapping setting, you will then need to choose where to place the image. One option is to simply drag the image to a new position. To do this, select the image, then place the cursor over the image. Next, click and hold the left mouse button. Then, move the image to its new location on the page.

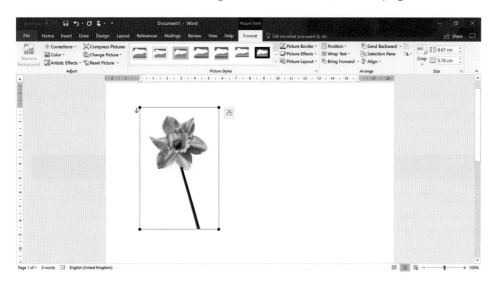

Activity 2.1

Open the document 'Flowers.docx' and insert the image 'daffodil.jpg' that your teacher has provided you with. Wrap the text around the image using the square text wrapping setting and place the image to the left-hand side of the text about daffodils. Double-check that the text is clearly wrapped around the image.

Activity 2.2

Move your cursor next to the word 'Tulip'. Now insert the image 'Tulip.jpg'. Wrap the text using the tight text wrapping setting. Drag the image across the page and position it to the right-hand side of the text about tulips. Make sure the text is wrapped around the whole outline of the image.

Activity 2.3

Insert the image 'Daisy.jpg'. Wrap the text using the through text wrapping setting and place the image to the right-hand side of the text about daisies. Edit the text wrap points to make sure that the text wraps around the white space in-between the daisies.

Save your document using the filename 'My_Flowers.docx'.

Cropping and resizing an image

You might find that you only want to use a particular part of an image. To remove the parts that you do not want, you will need to **crop** the image.

You might also find that an image you want to use is the wrong size. In this case, you will need to **resize** the image to change it to the correct size. You will also need to make sure that you do this correctly, maintaining the **aspect ratio** of the image.

To crop the image, select the image you want to use and you will see a **Format** tab appear. Select the **Format** tab and the **Crop** button. You will see thick black lines appear at the corners and the sides of the image.

Move the cursor to one of these lines then click and hold the left mouse button. You can now move the cursor across the image to crop it. You will be able to see which part of the image will be removed as a darker area will appear over that part of the image.

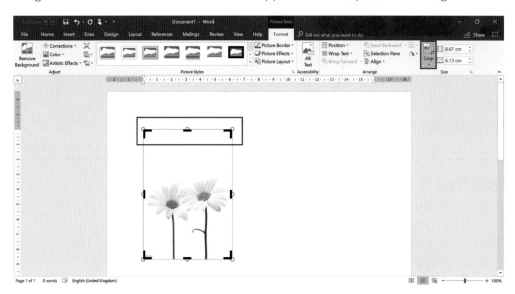

To resize an image, first, select the image. You will see dots appear in the corners and on the sides of the image. Move the cursor to one of the dots, then click and hold the left mouse button. You can now move the cursor towards, or away from, the image to make it larger or smaller.

To maintain the aspect ratio of the image, make sure that you use one of the dots in a corner to resize the image rather than one of the dots on the side of the image. If you do not maintain the aspect ratio of an image, it will look poorly designed and will appear distorted.

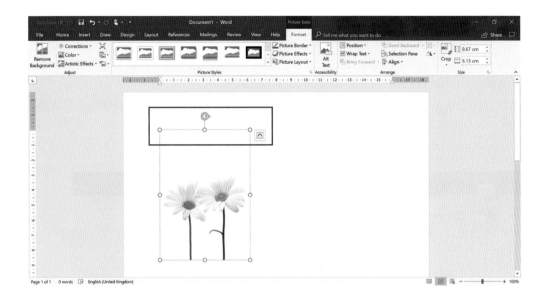

Activity 3.1

Open a new Microsoft Word document. Insert the image 'Daisy.jpg'.

Crop the image so that it only includes one daisy, not two.

Activity 3.2

Resize the image so that it fills the page. Make sure that you maintain the aspect ratio. Save your changes.

Skill 4

Inserting a table

One of the most important things about creating a document is the way you choose to present the information. One way of presenting information to make it clearer and easier to understand, is to put it in a **table**. A table means that data can be grouped together and given a title, to allow the audience to see the information clearly.

To create a table, you should:

1 Move your cursor to the place that you want to create a table.
2 Click on the **Insert** tab and click on the **Table** button.
3 You will see a menu appear and at the top of the menu will be a grid of squares. You will need to think about how many rows and columns you are going to use for the data in your table.
4 Move the cursor to the square in the top left corner. You should see an orange outline appear around this square.

> **Key term**
>
> **Table:** a layout with boxes that can be used to make text easier to read.

5   Move the cursor to the right across the grid then choose and select the correct number of columns that you need for your table.

6   When you have selected the columns, move the cursor down the grid and choose the correct number of rows that you need for your table.

7   When you have selected a grid with the correct number of rows and columns, click the left mouse button.

You should now see a table appear in your document.

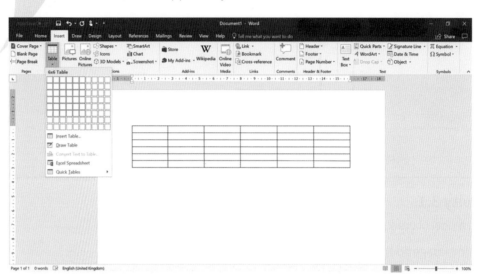

Tip

Don't forget to include a row for the titles in your table.

Key term

Cell: a small space in a table or spreadsheet where you can input your data.

Typing text into the table

1   Click inside the **cell** where you want the text to appear.

2   You can now start typing and the text will appear in that cell.

3   You will find that if the text you type is longer than the cell in the table, the cell will automatically change in length to make the text fit in the cell.

Adding an extra column to your table

1   Click inside the cell within the table, next to where you want to add the column.

2   You can add a column to the right of the cell or to the left of the cell.

3   Click on the **Layout** tab and click on the **Insert Left** or **Insert Right** button.

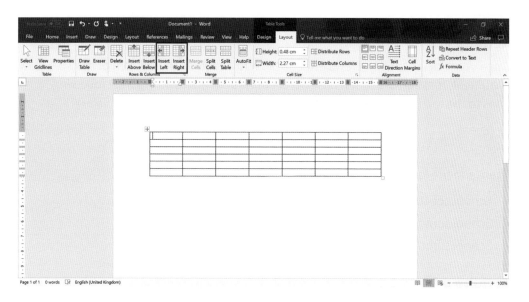

Adding an extra row to your table

1 Click inside the cell within the table, next to where you want to add the new row.

2 You can choose to add a new row above or below the cell.

3 Click on the **Layout** tab and click on the **Insert Above** or **Insert Below** button.

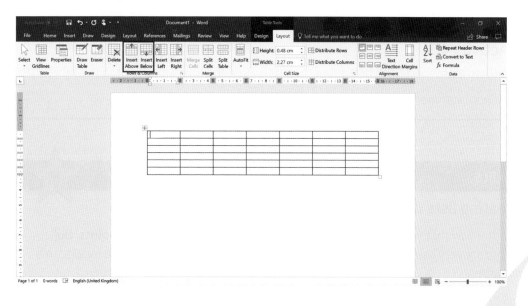

Activity 4.1

Open your document 'My_Newsletter.docx'. Add a table at the bottom of the document, making sure that it has two columns and four rows. Add the following titles to the top row in the table:

- 'Event'
- 'Date'

Then, add the following three events to the table:

- School sports day, 1st June
- School summer show, 25th June
- School summer picnic, 5th July

Activity 4.2

Add an extra column to the end of the table. Add the title 'Cost' to the column. Add the following information to the column, with one item on each row:

- Free entry
- $5 entry fee
- $4 for each person

Activity 4.3

Add an extra row to the bottom of the table. Type the following event to the table:

'School summer charity walk, 10th July, $5 for each person'.

Skill 5

Creating lists using bullet points

Another way that you can present information clearly is by using **bullet points**. Bullet points are very useful when you have **lists** of information that you want to include in a document.

It is much easier to read the list when each item is given a bullet point and a separate line in the document. It is more difficult to read the list as part of a text paragraph.

For example, if you need to be able to read a list of types of fruit, which of the following would be easier to read?

Apple, pear, orange, grapes, melon, apricot, banana, cherry, strawberry, blueberry and blackberry.

or

- Apple
- Pear
- Orange
- Grapes
- Melon
- Apricot
- Banana
- Cherry
- Strawberry
- Blueberry
- Blackberry.

Creating a bulleted list

1 Type each piece of information within your list on a separate line.
2 Select all of the items on the list.
3 Click on the **Home** tab.
4 Click on the **Bullets** button in the **Paragraph** section.

You should then see a bullet point appear at the beginning of each item in the list. The bullet point that normally appears on-screen will look like a small dot.

Changing the shape of the bullet point

1 Select all of the items in your list.
2 Click the arrow next to the **Bullets** button.
3 You will now see a selection of bullet point shapes that you can use.
4 Click on the bullet point shape that you want to change your design to and you will see the bullet points on your list change to that particular shape.

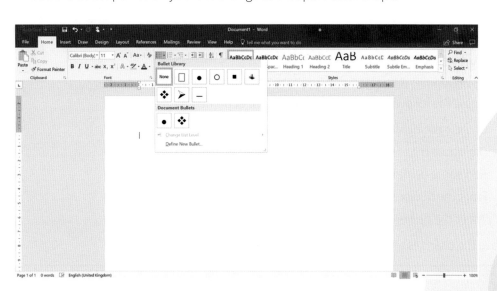

You can also use numbered bullet points rather than a specific shape. You can add numbered bullet points in the same way that you added shaped bullet points but you will need to click on the **Numbering** button instead of the **Bullets** button.

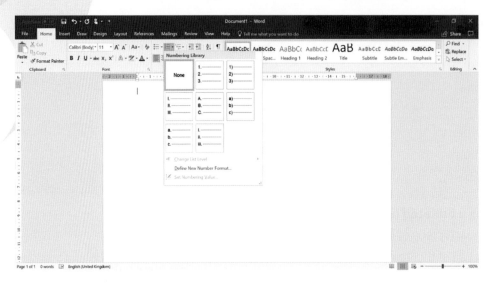

Activity 5.1

Open your document 'My_Flowers.docx'. Add the following sentence to the top of the document:

'The flowers that are included in this document are:'

Then, add a bullet point list of the three flowers that are included in the document.

Activity 5.2

Change the bullets on your bullet point list to the following shape:

Activity 5.3

Add a numbered bullet point list to the bottom of the document. Do this by changing the following list into numbered bullet points:

- Choose the right place in your garden for your flower.
- Dig a hole big enough for the flower to fit in.
- Add some compost to the hole.
- Plant the flower and fill the hole again.
- Water the flower.

Save the changes to your document.

Skill 6

Adding a header and footer

Headers and **footers** are added to a document to provide additional information about the document. A header is added to the top of a document and a footer is added to the bottom. This should be easy to remember given their names! When added, a header and a footer will be displayed on every page of your document.

A header can be used to add the filename of the document and the author name to the document as well. Sometimes the version of the document is also included in the header, such as 'Final draft'.

A footer can be used to add information, such as the date and the page number of the document.

Key terms

Header: the section at the top of a document.

Footer: the section at the bottom of a document.

Adding a simple text header

1   Click on the **Insert** tab and then click on the **Header** button.
2   You will see a menu with a list of header options.
3   Choose the option with the title: 'Blank'.

This should create a section at the top of the page that is separated by a dotted line and includes a small label with 'Header' written on it.

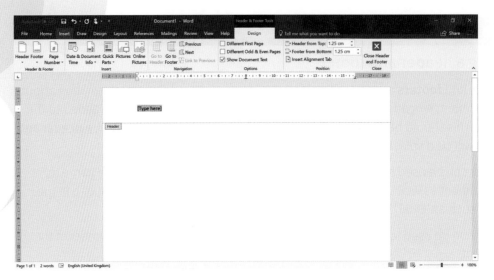

You can add information to the header in two ways:

1 You can simply type text into the header starting from where it says: [Type here].

2 You can also add specific information about the document, using the information options (detailed below).

Adding information about the document to the header

1 Click on the **Document Info** button.

2 You will see a menu of information that you can add.

3 Click on a menu option, such as 'Author', and the author's name will be added to the document in the header.

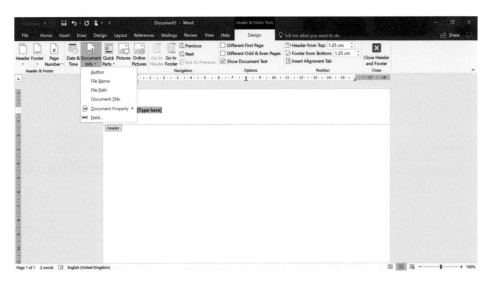

Adding a simple text footer

1 Click on the **Insert** tab.

2 Click on the **Footer** button.

3 You will see a similar list of options to adding a header.

4 Choose the 'Blank' option.

This should create a section at the bottom of the page that is separated by a dotted line and includes a small label with 'Footer' written on it.

You can type information directly into the footer or you can use the information options again.

Adding a page number for each page within the document

1 Click on the **Design** tab in Header & Footer Tools tab.

2 Click on the **Page Number** button to open the menu.

3 Choose 'Bottom of Page'.

4 Then choose from the list of options where you want the page number to appear in the footer.

Click on the selected option and the page number will be added to the footer.

To add the date and time to the footer, you should:

1 Click on the **Design** tab in Header & Footer Tools tab.

2 Click on the **Date & Time** button.

A window will appear, detailing all the different ways that the date can be displayed within the footer: this is called the format. Now you should:

1 Choose a format for the date and/or the time.

2 Click on the format and the date and/or the time will appear within the footer of the document.

When you are happy with the information that you have added to the header and the footer, you will then need to click on the **Close Header and Footer** button.

Activity 6.1

Open your document 'My_Flowers.docx'. Add a header to the document that displays your name and the filename of the document.

Activity 6.2

Add a footer to the document that displays the page number and the date of the document.

Skill 7

Adding columns

You might want to use a document to create a news article or feature. You might also want to make the lines of text shorter and easier to read. One way that you can do this is by using **columns** within your document.

A document normally includes one single column, that stretches the text across the page, from one side to the other. However, you can change the page layout to display the text in more than just one column. This can make your document look a bit more like a magazine or newspaper article, or it can simply make the lines of text shorter and easier to read.

To change the text so that it sits within two columns, you will need to:

1. Select the text that you wish to convert into more than one column.
2. Click on the **Layout** tab and the **Columns** button.

The column menu will now appear, allowing you to choose how many columns you would like to separate the text out into. Next, you need to select the number of columns that you wish to include.

You should now see that your text has been split into the number of columns that you have chosen.

You can also add an additional formatting technique to the columns to make them look neater. If you look at the right edge of each column, you will notice that all the lines of the text finish in different places. They don't all appear in a neat line, like they do in the left-hand side of the column. You can use an additional formatting technique to make the right-hand side of the column into a neat line as well! This is called 'justifying the text'.

To justify the text, you should:

1. Select the text.
2. Click on the **Home** tab and the **Justify** button in the **Paragraph** section.

You will now see that the text appears in a neat line down the right-hand side of the column as well. This formatting technique spaces the text out in the column to create this straight line.

> **Key term**
>
> **Justify:** the text is evenly spaced between the left and right-hand margins of the page.

Activity 7.1

Open the document 'School_News_Article.docx' that your teacher has provided you with. Change the text within the article so that it is split into three columns, then justify the text within the columns.

Using page formatting options

An important part of creating a new document is the way it appears within the **page setup**. It is very important that it looks formal and well presented. There are a number of formatting options that you can use to make sure that your document looks formal.

Page orientation

The first thing that you could do to alter your page layout is to change the **orientation** of your document, or even just a single page of the document. The 'orientation of a page' simply means the way the page is displayed. There are two types of orientation: portrait and landscape.

The portrait orientation is how a page is usually displayed on-screen. This is when the longest two sides of the page appear on the left- and right-hand side.

The landscape orientation is when a page is displayed the opposite way round, meaning when the longest two sides of the page run along the top and the bottom of the page.

You can change the orientation of a document, or even a single page, from portrait to landscape, to help things fit easily on the page.

The landscape orientation can be very useful when you have a large image and text that you need to display side-by-side. It can also be very useful when you are including a table of data that has a lot of columns.

To change the orientation of a whole document, you need to:

1 Click on the **Layout** tab and click on the **Orientation** button. This will give you the option of using either portrait or landscape.

2 Select which orientation that you would like to use for your document.

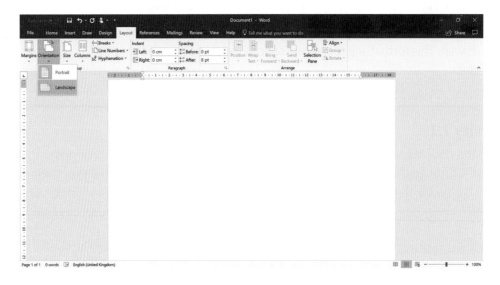

Key terms

Page setup: this is how the page will be displayed. It includes settings such as orientation.

Orientation: the direction in which a page is displayed. This can be portrait or landscape.

To change the orientation of a single page in a document, you should:

1 Select all of the text on the page.
2 Click on the **Layout** tab.
3 Click on the small arrow at the bottom right-hand corner of the page setup area.

This will open a window detailing additional page settings.

Next, you will need to:

1 Click on the arrow at the end of the 'Apply to' box. This means that the settings will be applied to the Whole document.
2 Change this option to 'Selected text'.
3 Click Portrait or Landscape to choose an orientation.

This will alter the orientation of the page that contains the selected text.

Page margins

You will notice that if you look at a document page, there is white space around all of the edges. This is because the text is set to be displayed at a specified distance from the edge of the page. This is called the **margin**.

Sometimes, you might have a lot of information that you wish to fit onto a page. In order to create a little more room on the page itself, you could alter the margins.

To alter the margins, you should:

1 Click on the **Layout** tab and click the **Margins** button. A menu will appear, showing you different margin options.

2 Change the margin options from 'Normal' to 'Narrow' to create a little more room on the page.

You should now be able to see the text move closer to the edges of the on-screen page. This will create a little more room on the page for you to add more text.

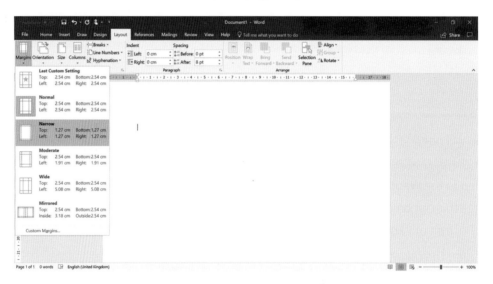

Line spacing

Sometimes, when you create a document, especially for school, your teacher might want you to leave extra room between the lines of text on the page. This is so that they can write their comments about how you can improve on your writing technique. It is difficult to do this when the lines of text are very close together.

You can add **line spacing** by using a formatting technique to move the lines of text further apart, making additional room for your teacher to write comments. This formatting option is called line spacing.

Changing the line spacing of the text within a document

1   Select the text that you want to amend.

2   Click on the **Layout** tab and click on the small arrow at the bottom right-hand corner of the 'Paragraph' section. This will open a window that lists a number of formatting options.

3   In the 'Spacing' section, change the line spacing option from 'Single' to 'Multiple'.

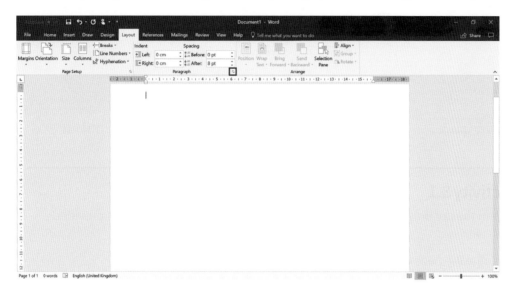

You can also change the line spacing to either '1.5 lines' or 'another value'. The '1.5 lines' setting will create half a line of space between the lines and 'Double' lines will create a whole blank line space between the lines of text.

Page border

To add finishing touches to your document, you might wish to add a **border** to each page. This can make the document stand out and appear as though it is well-designed. However, you should make sure that the border is nice and simple, or it might distract from the purpose of the document.

Adding a border to the pages in your document

1   Click on the **Design** tab and click the **Page Borders** button. This will open a window of options for a page border.

2   Change the setting to 'Box', 'Shadow' or '3-D'.

3   Choose a style of border in the style section.

4   When you have changed the setting and have chosen a particular style of border, click on 'OK'.

You should now see the border appear on each page.

> **Key term**
>
> **Border:** a line that can be placed around an image or a block of text.

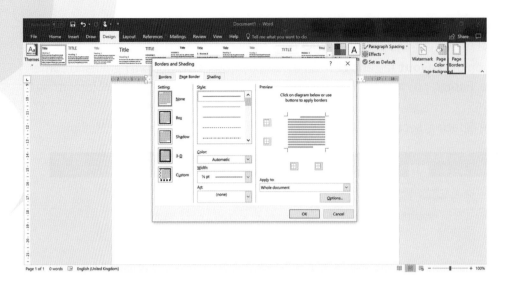

Activity 8.1

Open the document 'School_News_Article.docx' that your teacher has provided you with.

Change the page orientation to landscape.

Activity 8.2

Make the page margins in the document smaller.

Activity 8.3

Change the line spacing in the document for the bottom paragraph of text to 1.5 spacing.

Activity 8.4

Add a border to the document.

Skill 9

Using print preview

When you have completed your document, you might want to see what it will look like when it is printed. It is difficult to see this in the 'Normal' view on-screen as you can usually only see sections of the page at any given time. There is a view setting that you can use to see the whole page before you go to print the document. This is called the **Print Preview**.

Viewing a page in Print Preview

1   Click the **File** tab and click the 'Print' option.

2   You will see a window appear. In that window, you should be able to see the whole page of the document.

3   You can use the arrows at the bottom of the window to view additional pages in the document, if there is more than one page.

Activity 9.1

Open your document 'My_Flowers.docx' again. View the document in Print Preview.

Scenario

Staying safe when using the internet

Your school has created a leaflet that it wants to give out to all parents, inviting them to an event at the school talking about the internet and internet safety. The event will teach them all about how to stay safe when they or their children are using the internet and some of the issues that they might find when using the internet.

Activity 1

Open the document 'Internet_Leaflet.docx' that your teacher has provided you with. Look at the information about the event, detailed within the leaflet.

Activity 2

Insert the image: 'internet1.jpg' into the document and choose a suitable text wrap for it.

Activity 3

Insert a table into the document and add the following information:

- 10th July, 3:30pm until 5pm
- 16th July, 3:30pm until 5pm
- 20th July, 12:30pm until 2pm

Activity 4

Insert the following list into the document, using bullet points:

Viruses and malware, Social media, Using the internet for research, Playing games

Activity 5

Change the page orientation to landscape and make the margins smaller. You could move the text to make it fit the new page orientation more effectively. You could also format the text to make it look interesting for the intended audience.

Activity 6

Add a suitable border to the page, then view the page in 'Print Preview' before printing it to make sure that you are happy with the layout of the document, before printing.

Challenge 1

There are many additional tools and options that you can use in Microsoft Word. There are three more tools listed below that you can use to challenge yourself, when creating a formal-looking document.

Find and replace

There is a tool available called 'Find and Replace'. This can be very useful if there is a word that you want to change multiple times within a document. You might have spelt a particular word incorrectly multiple times within your document, or you might have changed your mind about using the word and want to replace it with a different word.

Using the Find and Replace tool

1 Click on the **Home** tab and then the **Replace** button, to open the 'Find and Replace' window.

2 In the top box displayed within the pop-out window, you can type in the word that you would like to replace.

3 In the bottom box within the pop-out window, you can type in the new word that will replace the old word.

> **WATCH OUT!**
>
> Be careful when using the 'Replace All' option as you might end up replacing parts of words rather than whole words.

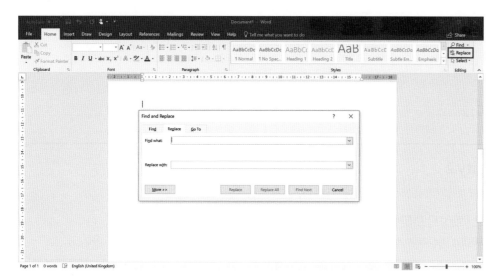

You can go through the document and replace each word separately, by clicking the 'Replace' option. Alternatively, you can replace all the words at once by clicking the 'Replace All' option.

> **Activity 1**
>
> Open your document 'My_Flowers.docx' again. Change all instances of the word 'Latin' to 'botanical'.

Challenge 2

Hyperlinks

Hyperlinks are a way of directing your audience to information in another place, such as another document or a website.

Creating a hyperlink

1 Select the word or words that you want to appear in the hyperlink

2 Click the **Insert** tab and the **Link** button in the **Links** section. This will open the hyperlink window.

3 If you want to hyperlink to another document, you will need to find and select that document within your files.

4 If you want to hyperlink to a webpage, type in the address of the webpage within the Address box at the bottom of the window.

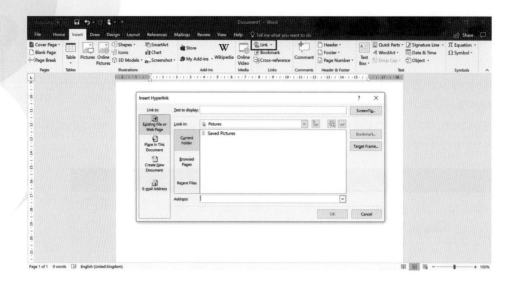

Activity 2

Add the following text to the bottom of the 'My_Flowers.docx' document:

- 'For more information about flowers, click here.'
- Insert a hyperlink to a website about flowers, using the words 'Click here'.

Challenge 3

Adding a cover page

Another way of making a document look formal is to add in a cover page. A cover page will tell your audience what the document is about. It can also attract their attention to the document, making them want to read it.

To add a cover page:

1 Click on the **Insert** tab then click on the **Cover Page** button. This will open a window that includes several choices of design for the cover page.

2 Click on the design that you wish to use so that the cover page will be added to the beginning of the document.

3 Change the text on the cover page to make sure your audience is clear on what the document is about.

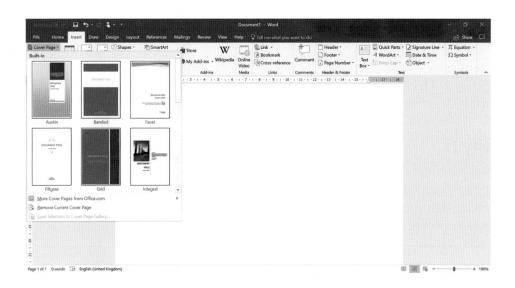

Activity 3

Add a cover page design that has flowers on it to the 'My_Flowers.docx' document. Change the title to 'All about flowers' and the subheading to your own name.

Final project – how to use the internet safely

At the internet event at your school, your teachers would like to give parents a small guide on how to use the internet safely. They have chosen some images and have also included some text that they would like to be added to the guide. They would like you to format the text to make it look more formal. They are relying on your excellent skills and experience in formatting documents to do this!

Activity 1

Open the document 'Internet_Leaflet.docx' as well as the images 'internet2.jpg' and 'internet3.jpg'. Think about how you could format the text and page layout using the formatting skills that you have acquired.

Activity 2

Use your experience of using formatting options to make the guide look well-designed and appealing to the parents attending the event. Look out for any information that you could add to a table as well as information that could be added to a bullet point list.

Reflection

1 Why is it important to make a document look formal?

_____

_____

_____

_____

_____

_____

2 How can you make certain information within the document clearer and easier to read?

_____

_____

_____

_____

_____

_____

3 Why is it important to maintain the aspect ratio of an image when it is resized?

_____

_____

_____

_____

_____

_____

4 What should you consider when you are creating a document for a particular audience and a particular purpose?

_____

_____

_____

_____

_____

_____

Multimedia for a purpose

	In this module, you will learn how to:	Pass/Merit	Done?
1	Create a plan for a presentation	P	
2	Recognise and select appropriate source materials	P	
3	Incorporate transition and animation	P	
4	Incorporate timings, audio and 'build' effects	M	
5	Demonstrate a clear sense of audience and purpose.	M	

Did you know?

More than 30 million presentations are created each day using Microsoft PowerPoint.

In this module, you are going to develop some essential skills that will help you to create high-quality multimedia presentations. The ability to create these high-quality presentations can be very useful for many career paths. In the workplace, you may need to present your findings from research, present sales figures for the year or present a new idea to your company.

The two most important things to consider when creating a presentation are:

1 audience (the people that will be viewing the presentation)

2 purpose (whether the presentation needs to inform, instruct, entertain, or a combination of all three).

You will need to make sure that the content and formatting that you choose is suitable for the intended audience and the purpose of the presentation. Any effects that you use, such as animations and slide transitions, should also be carefully considered with audience and purpose in mind.

The multimedia presentation that you are going to create, using Microsoft PowerPoint, in this module is for an information point at a zoo. Many people rely on information points in zoos, museums, galleries and theme parks to provide them with both interesting and important information.

You will also learn:

- how to create a master slide
- how to add narrations to slides
- how to use the slide show settings.

Before you start

You should:

- know how to add text to a slide and how to insert images
- know how to choose different layouts for a slide and how to format the content
- know how to use effective page design and how to create a presentation that meets the needs of the audience
- know how to create hyperlinks and how to use these to create non-linear presentation
- know how to use the internet to search for suitable images to include within a presentation
- be aware of copyright issues when using images found on the internet.

Introduction

Being able to create an effective multimedia presentation can be a very valuable skill to have. For example, in many different career paths and university courses, you might be asked to create a presentation to help provide information about yourself as well as information about certain products, services or topics.

Unfortunately, it is easy to make a number of mistakes when creating a **multimedia** presentation. You might add too many slide **transitions** or too many different **animations**, making the presentation confusing and unclear for your audience. If you learn how to correctly and effectively use multimedia elements, such as slide transitions and animations, this can make your presentation more appealing, more exciting and more formal.

You will start to learn how to use these elements effectively, in order to hold your audience's attention, rather than distracting or annoying them. This will also include being able to choose suitable transitions and animations, as well as learning how to create different **triggers** for these **effects**, such as different timings. You will also learn how to create a plan for a presentation, in the form of a **design specification**. All these skills will allow you to create an exciting and well-designed multimedia presentation.

Skill 1

Creating a design specification

In order to create a high-quality multimedia presentation, you will need to make sure that you plan it carefully first. One method you can use to plan your presentation is by using a design specification. A design specification is like a storyboard that you might create for an animation or a video. It allows you to detail the **content** that will appear on each slide, including the **layout** and **formatting** of that content.

A design specification also includes details of any slide transitions and animations, along with the triggers and timings for each one, or even the specific sound that needs to be played. It will also detail which slides need to be linked to other slides.

Layout: the way that text and images are arranged on a slide.

Formatting: changing the appearance of an image or text, such as changing its font type.

A design specification should include enough detail within it to allow a third party (someone else) to be able to create the presentation themselves, using the information that you provided in the design specification. This includes details surrounding the formatting of the fonts, the layout, the slide transitions, the animations and the links between each slide. By creating a design specification for your presentation, you are showing that you have planned it carefully, have thought about what it should look like and also what should be included within it. It is with careful planning that you can do your best work!

You will learn how to plan some of these elements within this Skill section, to enable you to add to your design specification as you learn new skills throughout the module.

Font

For the font used on each slide, you must give information about which font should be used, the size of the font, the colour of the font and any other styling that should be added such as bold, italics or underlining.

Layout

For the layout of each slide, you must provide information about where each item within the content is going to be placed on the slide. This includes the text, images and buttons. You must also provide information about any background colour or design that will be used on each slide.

Slide transitions and animations

For the slide transitions and animations for each slide, you must have information about the specific effect that will be used, as well as the duration, the trigger for it and the order in which animations should happen.

Arrows

Arrows need to be used between the slides to show which slides should be linked to other slides. This will also show where all the hyperlinks need to be link to.

You are now going to complete the font and layout sections of your design specification.

Activity 1.1

Open the file 'Design_Specification.docx' that your teacher will give you. This is a template for you to use to create a plan for a multimedia presentation.

Now open the file 'Design_Specification_Example.docx' as well. This is an example of how to complete the template and to show a design plan for a multimedia presentation.

Activity 1.2

You are going to create a plan for a presentation about your favourite things.
You will need to choose three of your favourite things to be included within your presentation. This could be your favourite food, favourite colour, favourite animal or any other of your favourite things.

Using the design specification template, create a plan for your presentation. At this point, you will only need to include the content, slide number, slide title, font and links sections.

Save your design specification as 'Design_Favourite_Things_v1.docx'.

Activity 1.3

Show your plan to a partner and ask them whether it clearly shows:

- the content that you want to include
- where the content should be placed on the slide
- fonts that should be used
- which other slides it should be linked to.

Activity 1.4

Using your design specification, create slides for your presentation about your favourite things. You will only need to add the content and links to each slide for the moment.

Save your presentation as 'My_Favourite_Things_v1.pptx'.

Activity 1.5

You are going to include a picture of yourself and your best friend in your presentation. Using a digital camera or mobile phone, ask a partner to take a picture of you and your best friend.

Key term

Ethical behaviour: behaving in a way that shows moral principles. It is seen as good and honest behaviour.

Key term

Audience: the people that will view the presentation.

As your friend will appear in the picture, even though the picture belongs to you, you will need to get their permission to use it for your presentation. Make sure your friend gives you their permission to use the photo. This is a good example of **ethical behaviour**.

Skill 2

Adding slide transitions

A slide transition is a type of animation that is used to help you move from one slide to the next. Slide transitions make presentations more interesting and help to hold the attention of your **audience**. Keeping the audience interested is vital if you want them to understand and absorb the content.

Remember, too many different slide transitions can be distracting, so it is best to only choose one or two different effects.

Make sure that the timings for your slide transitions are suitable so that you don't keep your audience waiting too long. Equally, moving through the slides too quickly can be difficult for the audience, as they won't be able to read the content in the given amount of time.

When you add a transition to a slide, it will be added to the start of the slide, so the transition will be played when the slide appears. You can select the slide that you want to add a transition to by clicking on the **Transitions** tab.

You can also see the full selection of slide transitions available by clicking on the ▼ arrow at the end of the slide transitions section. You will then see a large menu of the slide transitions.

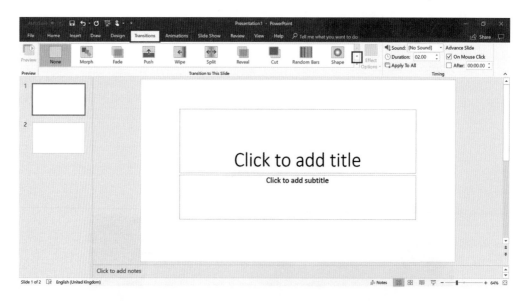

There are lots of transitions to choose from, so you may want to experiment with different ones until you decide which one you prefer. If you click on the button of the transition effect, you will see a preview of the effect in the main viewing pane (window). Remember, you will want to hold your audience's attention, but you won't want to overwhelm them with a transition that is too fancy.

Some of the slide transitions have an additional option to **customise** the transitions. You can locate these additional options by clicking the **Effect Options** button.

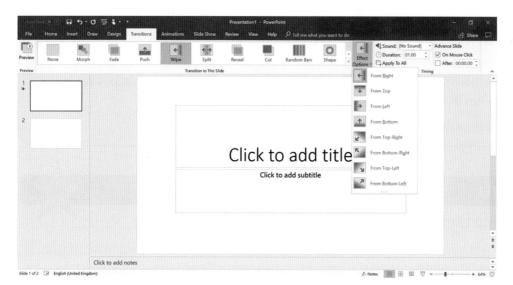

If you click the **Effect Options** button, for example, when you have the 'Wipe' transition selected, you will see that you can choose which direction the slide will wipe in from.

To see what your slide transitions look like, you can click the Preview button.

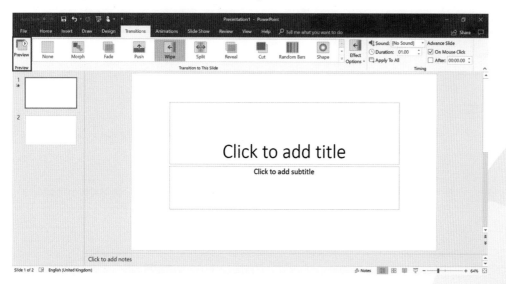

To check how your slide transition looks, as well as what it sounds like, click the **Preview** button.

Activity 2.1

Open your presentation file 'My_Favourite_Things_v1.pptx'. Add the slide transition 'Push' to your first slide, to make the slide appear as though it is coming out from the right of the screen.

Experiment with two other slide transitions on your first slide. Then, choose the one you like best. Remember to save your file.

Activity 2.2

Open your design file 'Design_Favourite_Things_v1.docx'. Complete the slide transitions section for each of your slides, to show which slide transitions you will use. You do not need to include any timings at this stage.

Save your design file.

Skill 3

Adding timings and audio to slides

When you have selected and added your slide transitions, you will need to make sure that they are not too fast or too slow. To do this, you will need to set a suitable timing for each one. A suitable timing would be between 0.5 and 1 second. Remember, you don't want to keep your audience waiting too long. The time taken for the slide transition is called the duration. You can type the time that you would like the transition to take, directly into the Duration box.

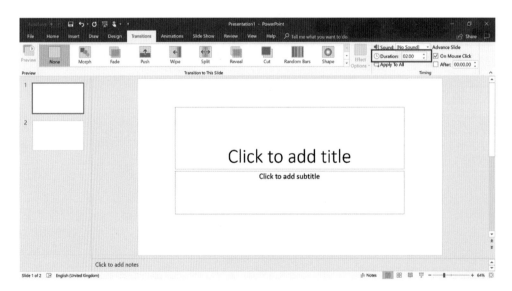

You can view the timing of the slide transition by clicking on the button for the transitions again. You can also click the **Preview** button which will also show you the slide transition.

To make your presentation look more well-designed, make sure that it is consistent in style by using the same transitions throughout the presentation.

When you have chosen a slide transition and duration that you are happy with, you can quickly apply it to all your slides by clicking the **Apply To All** button.

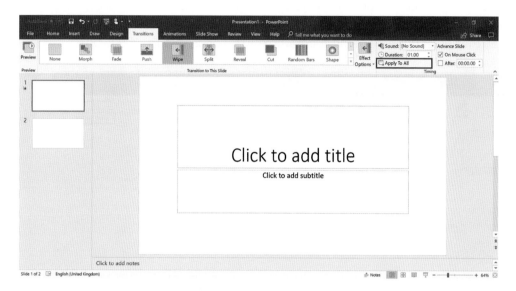

You can set the presentation to allow your audience, or the presenter, to move to the next slide by clicking on the mouse. You can also set the presentation to be **automated**. To do this, you will need to set a time for how long you want a slide to be displayed before the presentation will automatically move to the next slide.

You can also set both of these options in advance of your presentation (manually clicking, or automated). This can be very useful when a presentation is displayed at an information point within a venue. The presentation could be set to transition to the next slide after a certain amount of time, or it could be set to allow the audience to click on the screen and move to the next slide, before the timer has run out.

The setting to move from one slide to the next is called an 'Advance Slide'. To advance to the next slide by clicking the mouse or the screen (if you are using a touchscreen computer), you will need to click the 'On Mouse Click' box. A tick should be shown in this box if you wish to allow this setting.

Key term

Automated: this does not require a person who is viewing all the slides in a presentation to click on anything, as it all automatically happens instead.

If you want to set an amount of time for the slide to be displayed, before it automatically moves to the next slide, you will need to select a suitable time frame. One way to check how much time is needed for your audience to read the content on each slide, is to read the text on each slide yourself and check the length of time that it takes you to read it. You can then enter this time frame, for example 30 seconds, into the 'After:' box.

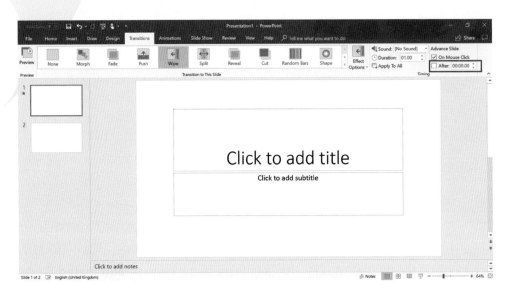

You could also add a sound effect to each slide transition. Again, you should remember that sound effects could be distracting for your audience, so you will need to choose them very carefully. It would not be practical to add a sound effect to each slide transition but using them occasionally to add interest can work well. For example, if you are going to reveal something interesting on the next slide, a drum roll sound effect might be very effective in attracting your audience's attention.

To add a sound effect to a slide transition, click the arrow at the end of the 'Sound:' box. You will then see a selection of sounds that you can choose from.

Activity 3.1

Open your presentation file 'My_Favourite_Things_v1.pptx'. Experiment with the timing of the slide transition on your first slide. Try setting it at 0.5 seconds, 1 second and 1.5 seconds. Decide which you think works best.

Activity 3.2

Open your design file 'Design_Favourite_Things_v1.docx'. Add timings to your slide transitions.

Activity 3.3

Open your presentation file 'My_Favourite_Things_v1.pptx' again. Add the slide transitions that you have designed to each slide within your presentation.

Activity 3.4

Set your presentation to be fully automated. The audience should not be able to click on the mouse to move to the next slide. Each slide should be displayed for 30 seconds.

Activity 3.5

Add a drum roll sound effect to the first slide of your presentation. Make sure that you include the drum roll sound effect in your design specification as well.

Save your presentation as 'My_Favourite_Things_v2.pptx'.

Skill 4

Adding animations

An animation is an effect that can be added to any item of content (text or image) on a slide. You can also use animations to make a presentation more interesting. We can all become easily bored by a mediocre (average) presentation, so anything you can use to attract the attention of your audience can help make the presentation more interesting.

Remember, you need to be careful about how you use animations in your presentation. For example, it might seem fun to include content that is whizzing all over the slide, but this can be very distracting for your audience. The audience are viewing the presentation because they want to learn about the content included within it. Therefore, you won't want to make this difficult for them by distracting them too much. If the audience has to follow the content around the slide with their eyes, it might make them feel very dizzy!

Think carefully about whether your animation has a **purpose**. You should only really use animations for two main reasons:

- to highlight a particular item of content within a slide
- to withhold content from your audience until the point at which you want them to see it.

To add an animation to some content on a slide, you will need to select the content first. When you have done this, click on the **Animations** tab.

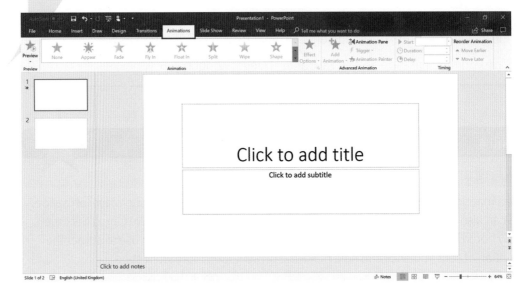

Choose a suitable animation for your content from the selection given. To see more animations, click the ▼ arrow at the end of the **Animations** section. You can also see this menu if you click on the **Add Animation** button.

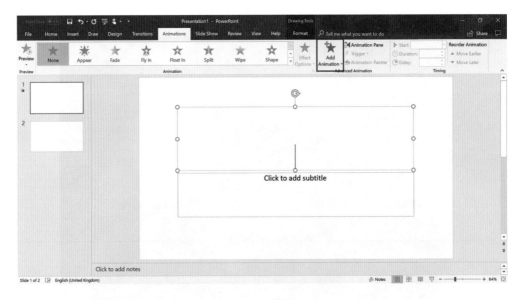

You will see that the animations are separated out into three sections: Entrance, Emphasis and Exit.

- *Entrance animations* are used to bring the content into the slide.
- *Emphasis animations* are used to make content that is already on the slide more obvious and to draw your audience's attention to it.
- *Exit animations* are used to remove the content from the slide.

You will need to choose a suitable animation, depending on what you want to do with the content.

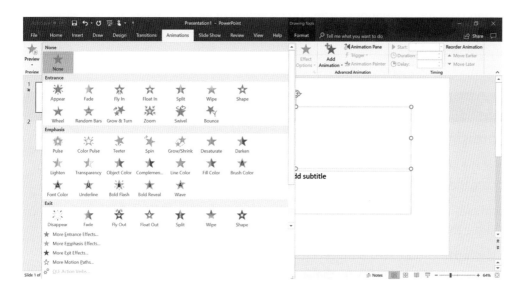

Activity 4.1

Open your presentation file: 'My_Favourite_Things_v2.pptx'. Find a slide in your presentation where you have included an image.

Add the 'Grow/Shrink' animation to the image. Then experiment with two other animations and decide which you like best.

Activity 4.2

Open your design file: 'Design_Favourite_Things.docx'. Identify which parts of the content from your presentation would be suitable to add an animation to. Remember, you do not want to add animations to everything as this will distract the audience too much. Only add animations to things that you want to stand out or be highlighted.

Activity 4.3

Open your presentation: 'My_Favourite_Things_v2.pptx'. Now add the animations that you have designed to your presentation.

Save your presentation as: 'My_Favourite_Things_v3.pptx'.

Activity 4.4

Ask a partner to look at the animations that you have added to your presentation. Ask them to think about whether you have:

- added animations to the right things
- added too many or too few animations
- added suitable animations for the presentation or whether they can suggest another animation style that would look better.

Skill 5

Customising animations and adding timings

Some of the animations have additional options to help you customise your slides. You can locate these by clicking on the **Effect Options** button.

For example, if you select the 'Fly In' animation and click on the **Effect Options** button, you will see that you can select which direction the content will 'fly in' from.

You will need to choose which triggers to use for your animation. To select what you want these to be, you can click on the arrow at the end of the 'Start:' box. This will give you three options: 'On Click', 'With Previous' and 'After Previous'.

- The 'On Click' option means that the animation will begin when the mouse is clicked on.
- The 'With Previous' option means that the animation will automatically begin with the previous animation that has been set.
- The 'After Previous' option means that the animation will automatically begin after the previous animation has played.

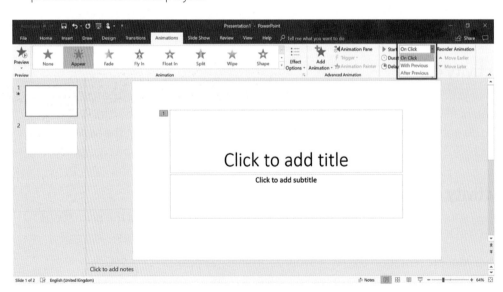

You will need to choose and select a suitable amount of time for your animation. If you make it run too fast, your audience might not see it happen at all. If you make it run too slowly, your audience might get frustrated waiting for the animation to finish.

To set the duration for your animation, type in the time, in seconds, into the 'Duration:' box. Again, a suitable time for entrance and exit animations would be between 0.5 to 1 second. For an emphasis animation, you will need to select a suitable amount of time to help you emphasise the content. This may depend on how long you want to draw your audience's attention to it.

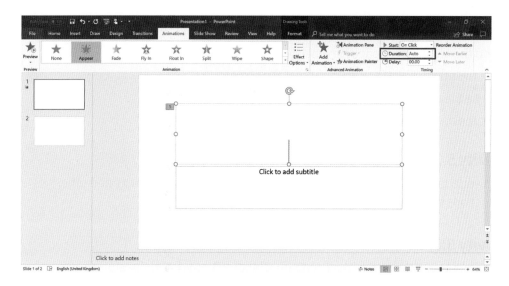

To see a clear view of all of the animations that you have set on your presentation content, you will need to open the animation pane.

To open the animation pane, click on the **Animation Pane** button. This will open it up on the right-hand side of the screen. It will provide a list of all the content that an animation has been set for, as well as the order in which the animations will happen. You can click on each item of content to see what animations have been set up. You can also quickly view which animations have been set up for each item of content by hovering over each one.

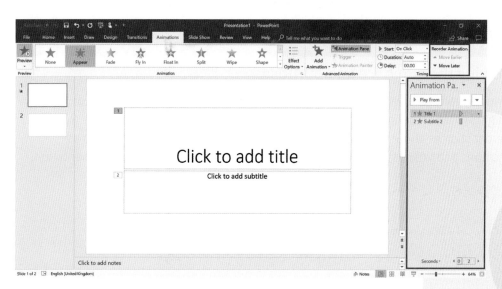

If you decide that the order in which your animations have been placed is incorrect, you can edit this easily by using the animation pane. Click on the item of content that does not appear in the correct place, then click on either 'Move Earlier' or 'Move Later' to move it to its correct location.

To view the animations that you have set up, click on the **Preview** button.

Activity 5.1

Open your presentation file 'My_Favourite_Things_v3.pptx'. Then do the following:

1 add the animation Float in to make your title appear on the first slide
2 set the title to Float in from the top of the screen
3 make the animation last 1 second
4 set the animation to begin when the mouse is clicked on.

Activity 5.2

Open your design file: 'Design_Favourite_Things_v1.docx'. Add timings and other instructions to customise your animations.

Activity 5.3

Open your presentation file 'My_Favourite_Things_v3.pptx'. Add the timings and customisations that you have designed, to your presentation.

Activity 5.4

With a partner, talk through the animations that you have added to your presentation and how you have customised each one. Explain why you think you have selected the best animation, in each instance.

Skill 6

Knowing the audience and purpose

You will already be aware that audience and purpose should be at the centre of your thoughts when creating a presentation. You will also understand that you can make different choices about both the content and the stylings of the content (such as transitions and timings) depending on the audience and purpose of your presentation.

Activity 6.1

Open your design file: 'Design_Favourite_Things_v1.docx'.

Who would you identify as the audience of your presentation?

What would you identify as the purpose of your presentation?

Activity 6.2

You now need to make your presentation suitable for a very young audience. The purpose of your presentation in this instance is to entertain your audience and make them laugh about your favourite things.

Make changes to your design file: 'Design_Favourite_Things_v1.docx', to make it suitable for this very young audience as well as its purpose.

Write a short paragraph at the end of your design specification, to explain the changes you have made so that it is suitable for the audience and its intended purpose.

Save your design file as: 'Design_Favourite_Things_v2.docx'.

Activity 6.3

Your presentation now needs to be changed so that it is suitable for an older audience. In this instance, the presentation is aimed at a prospective employer so that they can learn about your favourite things. It will need to look well-designed and formal.

Make changes to your design file: 'Design_Favourite_Things_v1.docx', to make it suitable for this new audience and intended purpose.

Write a short paragraph at the end of your design specification to explain the changes that you have made to your presentation, and to make it more suitable for the audience and its intended purpose.

Save your design file as 'Design_Favourite_Things_v3.docx'.

Scenario

You are going to the zoo!

The zoo is an exciting place to visit but you will need to let people know this in your presentation!

You are going to use your newly acquired skills to create a short presentation. The presentation will be emailed to members of the public, to entice them to visit a new zoo. The intended audience for the presentation are adults only.

Activity 1

Open the presentation file: 'Zoo_Advert.pptx' and the document 'Zoo_Design_Specification.docx' that your teacher will provide you with. The design specification is a complete design of what the presentation will look like. However, this particular presentation is incomplete. The content has been added to each slide but now you are going to need to add in the multimedia elements to the presentation.

Activity 2

Using the design specification, add the correct slide transitions into each slide. If you feel confident enough, you can also add in the timings as well.

Activity 3

Using the design specification, add the correct animations to each slide. If you feel confident enough, you could add in the timings and customise it as well.

Activity 4

Discuss with a partner why the transitions and animations that you have been asked to add in are suitable for the intended audience and how they make the presentation for the zoo more appealing.

Challenge 1

There are lots of additional skills that you can learn, relating to multimedia presentations. You are going to pick up three more skills in this section: how to create a master slide, how to add narration to your slides and how to use the slide show settings.

Creating a master slide

A master slide is a template. It allows you to define the layout and format settings that you want to use for each slide. This means that you do not need to manually apply these settings each time you create a new slide. If you use the master slide, the settings will automatically be applied. You can create more than one master slide in a presentation, to allow different layouts and formats to be repeatedly used in your presentation.

To create a master slide, click the **View** tab and select the **Slide Master** button.

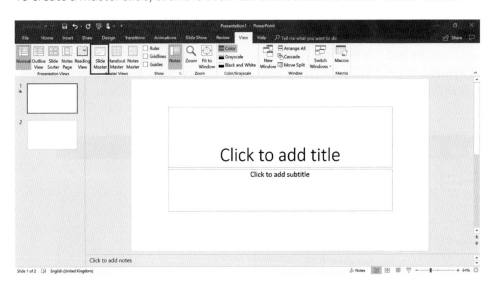

You will see that this creates a new tab called **Slide Master**. This tab includes lots of options relating to the master slide. You will also see a range of slide templates running down the left-hand side of the screen. You can customise these templates that already have some of the layout and formatting pre-set, or you can create your own template. It is easier to customise the templates that you have already been given.

Changing the layout of a template

You can change the layout of a template by simply moving the content boxes to the place on the slide where you want them to appear. If you want to include additional content boxes on a slide, then these are called placeholders. To insert a new placeholder, select the slide layout that you would like to add it to, then click on the **Insert Placeholder** button. This will give you a menu of different items that you can add to your slide.

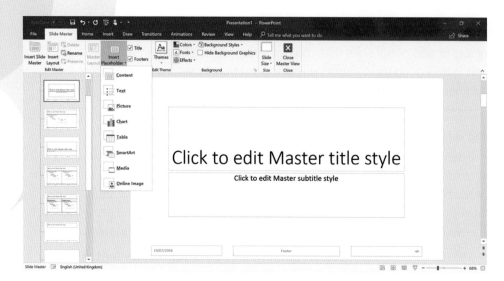

The presentation will automatically have a content box included for the title, text, date, slide number and footer. To quickly remove any of these items, click on the **Master Layout** button. This will make a menu appear that will show boxes ticked for each of the options. Click on the tick next to the content that you would like to remove.

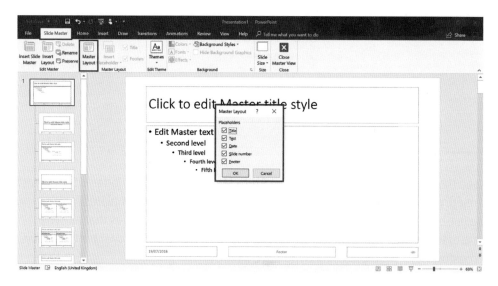

Setting a theme design

To set a theme design for the master slide, click on the **Themes** button and choose a theme. The design of the theme will be applied to the master slide.

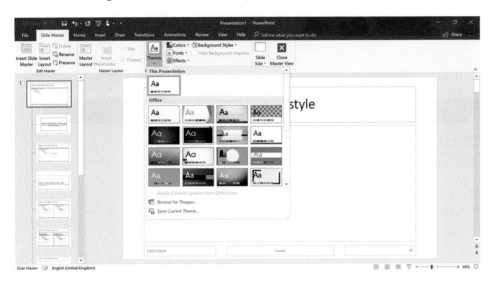

Setting a background

You can also set a background, rather than a theme, for your master slide.

Click on the **Background Styles** button and click on the option 'Format Background…' A format background pane will appear to the right of the screen. This will allow you to choose the fill that you would like to use for your background, along with the colour. It is automatically set as a solid fill.

To change the fill, click on the circle next to your choice of fill. To change the colour, click on the arrow next to the paint pot and select a colour. You should now see the background colour applied to your master side.

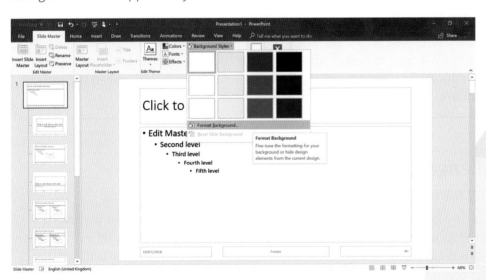

Changing the font

To change the font style of the text, select the text that you want to customise, such as the title. When you select the text, you will see a text formatting box appear. You can use the options in this box to change the font style, the font size and the font colour.

You can also change the alignment and add any further formatting to the font, such as setting it to bold. This means that each time you add a new slide to the presentation that includes a title, the settings that you have applied to the font will automatically be set.

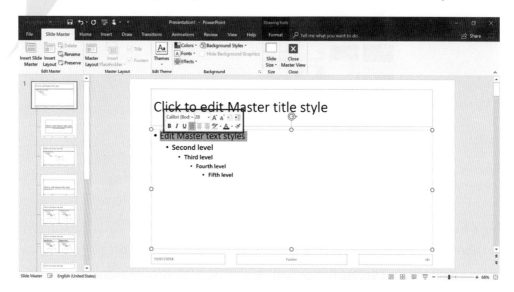

When you have finished creating your master slide, click on the **Close Master View** button. Each time you add a slide to the presentation, the master slide settings will be applied.

> ## Activity 1
>
> Create a master slide for the Zoo Advert presentation that your teacher has given to you. You will need to look at what formatting has been applied to the slides and include this within the master slide. This means that the master slide can be used in the future to add any other slides to the presentation.

Challenge 2
Adding narration to a slide

If your slide is going to be displayed, for example, at an information point, you might want to add some narration to the slide. This means that a voice recording will play when the slide is displayed. This is another great way to provide your audience with more information. To record narration for a slide, you will need to use a microphone.

You may want to plan out what you will say for the narration. You could write a short script for this. This is something that you could also include in your design specification.

When you are ready to record the narration, click the **Slide Show** tab and click on the **Record Slide Show** button. You can either set the narration to play from the beginning of the slide, or, if you select a particular slide that you would like narrated, you can set the narration to record from the current slide.

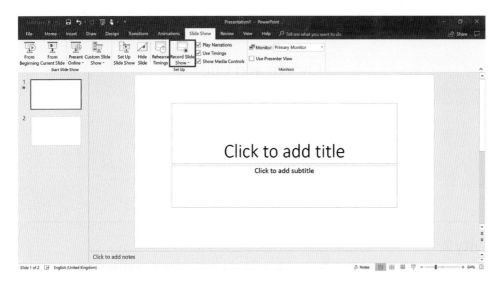

Once you have clicked on the **Record Slide Show** button, you will see the screen change to the slide recording screen. Click on the **Record** button at the top left-hand corner of the screen to begin recording your narration. You will see a countdown begin from 3 to 1. Wait for the countdown to begin before starting your narration. When you have finished your narration, click on the **Stop** button. To listen to your narration, click on the **Replay** button.

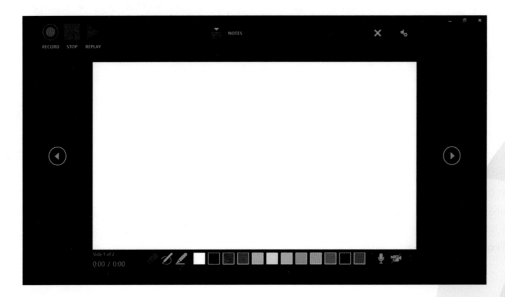

To make sure that your narration will begin playing when the presentation is viewed, make sure that the 'Play Narrations' box is ticked.

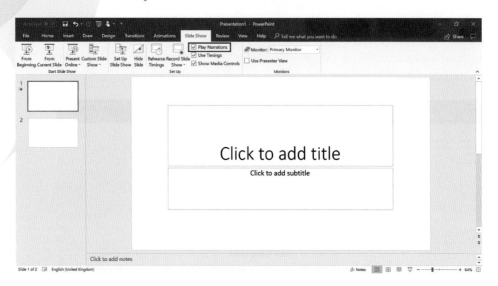

Tip

Remember, if you want the presentation to be fully automated, you will need to set timings for each slide.

Challenge 3

Using the slide show settings

When you have finished creating your impressive slide show, you will need to be able to allow your audience to view it.

The settings that you use for this will depend on how the presentation will be viewed by your audience. It could be used by a presenter who is using it within their own class, perhaps to help provide training for their audience. If this is the case, the presenter may want to be able to move the presentation to the next slide manually, when they have finished talking about the current slide. Therefore, they might simply require a setting that will allow them to run the slide show right from the beginning. To play the slide show from the beginning, click on the **Slide Show** tab and click on the **From Beginning** button.

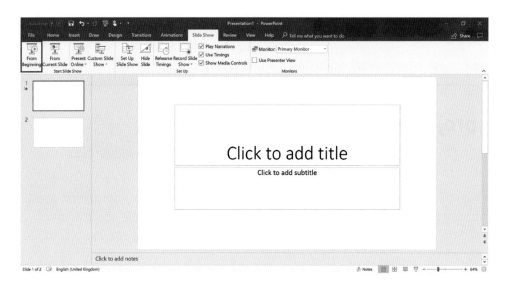

When you click on the **From Beginning** button, you will see that the first slide of the presentation appears on a full screen.

If the presentation is to be displayed at an information point, then it may require different settings. You may want to put the presentation into a setting called 'kiosk' mode. This will make the presentation into a full screen and will also make it continuously loop through the slides. To put the presentation into 'kiosk' mode, click on the **Show** tab and click on the **Set Up Slide Show** button.

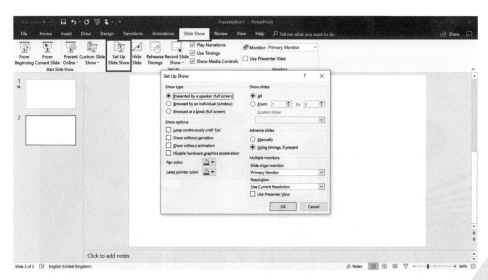

You will see a window appear that includes lots of different settings that can be changed. Under the 'Show type' section, click the circle next to 'Browsed at a kiosk'.

You should notice that this will automatically select the 'Loop continuously till Esc' option. This means that the presentation will loop back to the beginning again, to play again, when it reaches the end. If you are going to use the 'kiosk' mode, you will need to make sure that you have set timings for each slide.

Activity 4

Set the Zoo Advert presentation to be played in 'kiosk' mode.

Final project – welcome to our zoo

You are going to use all the skills that you have learnt here, to create a multimedia presentation for a zoo of your choice.

The zoo would like to use a presentation that they can display on their information point in the entrance to the zoo. They want the presentation to inform people about all the animals and the key facilities that are available at the zoo. They would also like you to include a quick quiz at the end of the presentation.

The zoo wants to make sure that all of the children attending the zoo understand the presentation. For this final project, the audience for the presentation is going to be 8 to-16-year-olds. You are going to use the internet to research information about zoos and find images for your presentation.

Stay safe!

When using the internet for research, make sure that you only use trusted websites.

WATCH OUT!

When you use content and images from the internet, always make sure that you add a reference that gives credit to the owner of the content. If you don't do this, then you are plagiarising their work.

Activity 1

Use the internet to research different zoos and choose one that you would like to base your presentation on. Choose suitable text and images that you could use in your presentation.

Your presentation must:

- include content suitable for the audience and its intended purpose
- be fully automated
- have a menu slide that includes a link to all the different sections in the presentation
- include a link on each slide directing it back to the menu slide.

Activity 2

Decide what you would like to include in your presentation and create a design specification to show this. Make sure that you include slide transitions and animations, including all their triggers and timings.

Activity 3

Create a multimedia presentation based on your design specification. You could challenge yourself by creating a master slide for your presentation to make it easier to create and add in additional slides in the future.

Activity 4

Write a report about your presentation for the zoo manager, explaining the choices that you have made while creating your presentation, and why it is now suitable for the audience and its intended purpose. You should comment on the content, the formatting, the slide transitions and the animations.

Activity 5

You could challenge yourself to add some narration to your presentation as well.

Tip

Remember, if you want to check your presentation to make sure that everything has been added correctly, you could compare it directly with your design specification. You could also challenge yourself by creating a testing table that includes all of the links, slide transitions and animations.

Reflection

1 Why are the audience and the purpose the most important things that you should consider when creating a presentation?

_____

_____

_____

_____

_____

_____

2 Why should you be careful to avoid adding in slide transitions that are too fancy?

_____

_____

_____

_____

_____

_____

3 How can animations be used to make a presentation more interesting?

_____

_____

_____

_____

_____

_____

4 Why is it important to create a design specification?

_____

_____

_____

_____

_____

_____

	In this module, you will learn how to:	Pass/Merit	Done?
1	Design a spreadsheet for a specific purpose	P	
2	Create the spreadsheet you have designed	P	
3	Test the spreadsheet you have created	P	
4	Modify the spreadsheet to make it suitable for its purpose	M	
5	Evaluate your spreadsheet.	M	

In this module, you will use your newly acquired skills to set up a brand new Microsoft Excel spreadsheet for your final project. This will involve designing a spreadsheet to plan a holiday. It will include deciding which data you will need to store within the spreadsheet and also which formulas you will need to use. Once you have created your spreadsheet, you will need to test it to prove that it works. You will then finish the project by evaluating your spreadsheet.

You will also learn:

- how to use conditional formatting
- how to use the goal seek function.

Key terms

Data: this is the data that the spreadsheet will store and use to perform calculations.

Formula: this is a rule that tells the computer what to do with the data. It has symbols or words, for example + or – or SUM. Formulas always begin with the = symbol. Two examples are =10+2 and =SUM(A1:B1).

Formulas: this is the plural of formula. It means more than one formula.

Design brief: a description of a system. This is used to create a design for a system.

Test: making sure a system works by trying to use different pieces of data in it.

Model: a system where you can change data to see what happens.

System design: the plan of what a system will do and how it will work.

Before you start

You should:

- know what a spreadsheet is and why it is used to store **data**
- be able to add data to a spreadsheet
- be able to enter a **formula** into a spreadsheet using symbols and functions such as +, -, *, /, SUM, AVERAGE
- be able to change a value in a spreadsheet and see which other values change
- be able to create a graph in a spreadsheet.

Introduction

A spreadsheet is a structured method of storing data. It lets you enter **formulas** to perform calculations. You can also use it to create graphs. When you work through the skills listed here, you will learn how to create a new spreadsheet from a **design brief**, including how to implement the design from the brief and to **test** how it works. Finally, you will evaluate your spreadsheet against your original design.

A spreadsheet can be used to **model** data. By changing the data in a spreadsheet, you can see what would happen without actually having to make it happen. This is called modelling.

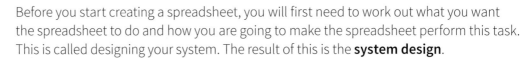

Skill 1

Designing a spreadsheet

Before you start creating a spreadsheet, you will first need to work out what you want the spreadsheet to do and how you are going to make the spreadsheet perform this task. This is called designing your system. The result of this is the **system design**.

To plan your spreadsheet, you first need a **scenario**:

You have just finished reading about a new games console that you would like to buy. However, you will need a spreadsheet to calculate how long it will take you to save up enough money to buy it. You receive a set amount of pocket money each week.

In this module the examples for each skill will show you how to set up a spreadsheet to calculate how long it will take you to save for a games console. You will need to work through these instructions to understand how they work.

You will also create a new spreadsheet for Ultimate League – a computer gaming competition in the activities for each Skill.

Objectives
Record how much pocket money you receive each week. Then record how much the games console will cost you. Calculate how long it will take you to save up enough money to buy the games console.

Data:

- weekly pocket money
- cost of games console
- amount you spend each week
- number of weeks needed to save for the games console.

Formulas:

- amount saved each week = (weekly money – money spent each week)
- number of weeks = cost of games console / amount saved each week.

Key terms

Scenario: a description of a situation, such as a description of what the spreadsheet will do.

Objective: a goal that you are aiming to achieve.

Activity 1.1

Ultimate League is a computer game competition and people pay a fee to enter the competition.

There are three cash prizes for winners ($1000 for 1st place, $500 for 2nd place, $200 for 3rd place).

Last year, 280 people entered the Ultimate League competition. The company who created the competition want to work out how much they need to charge each person to enter the competition, to make sure they will at least break even (meaning they earn as much as they spend).

On a piece of paper, write down the objectives for this spreadsheet.

Activity 1.2

On the paper, write a list of all the data that will need to be entered into, and calculated by, the spreadsheet.

Activity 1.3

On the paper, write down the formulas that you will need to use to complete the spreadsheet.

Don't worry if you don't know what they all are yet. A design develops as you create your system. It is ok not to know everything from the very start.

Tip

+ equals addition
– equals subtraction
/ equals division
* equals multiplication

Skill 2

Create the layout

You will need to decide how your spreadsheet is laid out.

You can design the layout on paper first or alternatively, use the spreadsheet straight away.

First, look at your list of data. This will tell you the information you need to store. Each piece of data needs a label and space for the data.

Now look back at the games console scenario in **Skill 1**.

The design identifies the following data as being required:

- weekly pocket money
- cost of games console
- amount you spend each week
- number of weeks you need to save for the games console.

Create a label for each piece of data.

Tip

You could do these activities in your own currency.

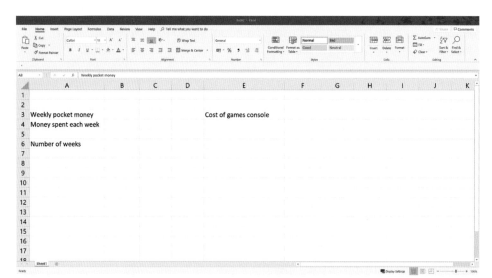

Enter an example of the data next to each label. The data listed here is just an example as you might receive more or less pocket money. Additionally, your games console might cost more or less than the one listed here.

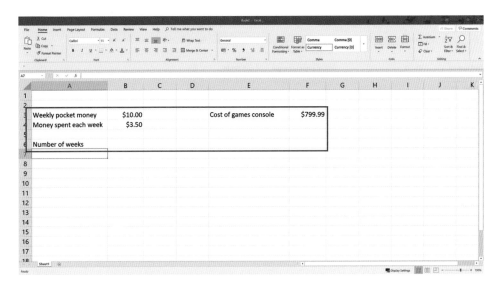

If the data is going to be listed as money, then change the data type to currency. Click on the cell you want to change, then click on the **Currency** button on the menu.

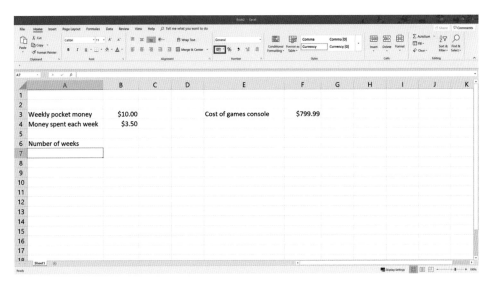

The formula for Number of weeks already has a label here. The formula needs a label to work out the amount saved each week.

You can then add a label for Amount saved per week.

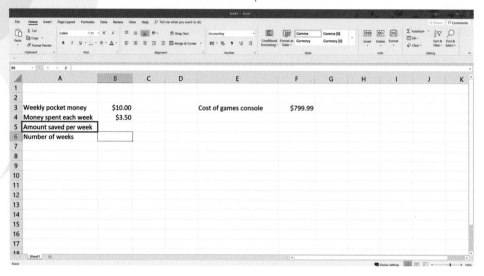

Activity 2.1

Create a new spreadsheet for the Ultimate League from **Skill 1**, using Microsoft Excel.

Add labels for the data that you have identified in **Activity 1.2.**

You should include:

- first prize cost
- second prize cost
- third prize cost
- number of entries
- entry cost.

Remember to save your spreadsheet using a sensible name.

Activity 2.2

Add the following data for the labels you have entered:

- first prize cost = $1000
- second prize cost = $500
- third prize cost = $200
- number of entries = 280
- entry cost = $10.

Remember to save this data to your spreadsheet.

Activity 2.3

Add labels for the formulas that you identified in **Activity 1.3**.

This should include:

- total prize money
- total income (Number of entries * entry cost)
- money made (Income – prize money).

Remember to save your spreadsheet.

Skill 3

Entering the formulas

Now that you have your layout set out, you will need to enter the formulas into the spreadsheet. You already have a good idea of what these will be from your design.

Remember:

- each formula starts with an =
- click (or type) the cell references for each formula
- the Amount saved per week has the formula: =B3–B4.

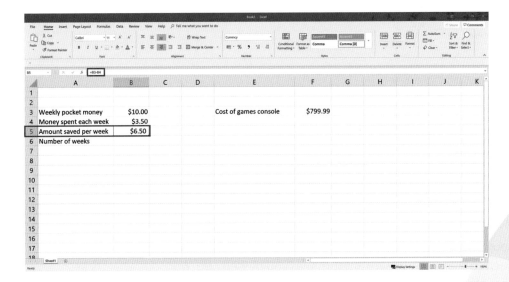

The Number of weeks is required is the cost of the console divided by the amount saved each week:

=F3/B5

Tip

You might get lots of numbers after the decimal point, for example 123.0753846 weeks. You do not need that many numbers!

Click on the cell, then the **Decrease decimals** button to reduce the number of decimal places shown.

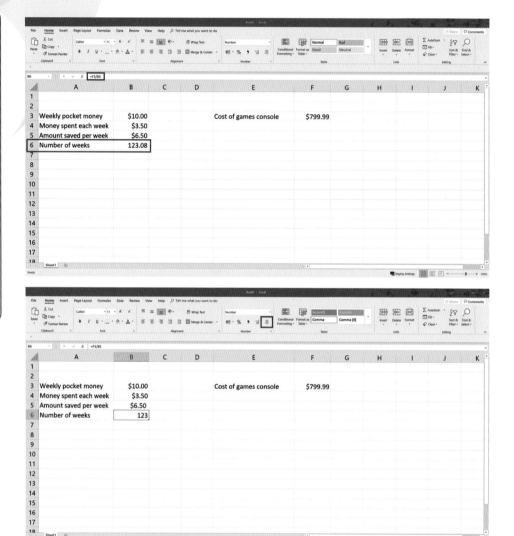

Activity 3.1

Look back at the formulas you thought you would need earlier - do any of these need to change? Are there any formulas you missed out? Work out what these changes, and/or new formulas are.

Activity 3.2

Open your Ultimate League spreadsheet.

Enter a formula to work out the Total prize money. This is the First prize + Second Prize + Third Prize.

Add a label for the total prize money if you don't already have one.

Activity 3.3

In the Ultimate League spreadsheet, enter the formula to work out the Total income.

This is the Number of competitors * entry cost.

Activity 3.4

In the Ultimate League spreadsheet, enter the formula to work out the Money made. This is the Total income minus the total prize money.

Tip

These three cells are next to each other, so you could use the SUM function.

Skill 4

Testing your spreadsheet

When you create a spreadsheet, or any system, you will need to make sure that it works. If it does not work, then the information you get from it will be inaccurate. This could lead you to make some bad decisions because you are using incorrect information.

When using formulas, you will need to test whether they are correct, meaning that they give you the correct result. You can do this using the following steps:

- Step 1: Identify what you are going to test, for example, which formulas you are going to test.
- Step 2: Identify how you are going to test them.

You could:

- check that the result is correct by working it out another way (such as using a calculator)
- change the values used in the formulas, to make sure the result changes as well.

If the results from Step 2 show that the formulas are working, that's great – well done!

If the results from Step 2 show that something doesn't appear to be working, then that's ok too! You just need to work out what is wrong with the formulas and then fix it. Nobody gets everything correct first time.

In the Games Console spreadsheet, there are two formulas that can be tested:

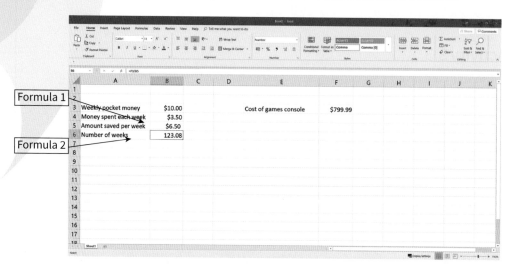

A table can help you structure your tests, this called a test table.

These are the values that are used in the formula you are testing.

Formula being tested	Cell being tested	Data input	Expected result	Did it work?
1	B5	B3 = $10.00 B4 = $3.50	$6.50	Yes
2	B6	B5 = $3.50 F3 = $799.99	229	Yes

These tested if the formulas work with the current values. What about if you change the values?

Create a table and put in new data input values. Work out what the result should be – then change the values in the spreadsheet and see if it works.

Formula being tested	Cell being tested	Data input	Expected result	Did it work?
1	B5	B3 = $15.00 B4 = $3.50	$11.50	Yes
2	B6	B5 = $11.50 F3 = $500.00	43	No

The last test did not work.

This is ok! We just need to work out why.

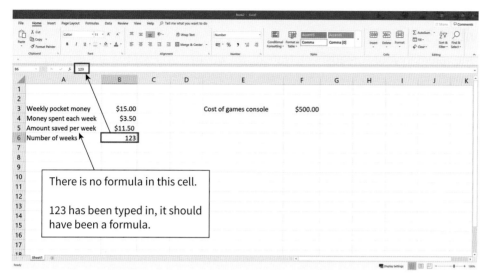

Fix the error and then do the test again!

Formula being tested	Cell being tested	Data input	Expected result	Did it work?
2	B6	B5 = $11.50 F3 = $500.00	43	Yes

Activity 4.1

Create a test table for your Ultimate League spreadsheet.

Activity 4.2

Type the cell reference of each formula into your spreadsheet, in a new row within your table.

You should have the following formulas displayed:

- Total prize money
- Total income
- Money made.

Activity 4.3

Write the data values that will appear in your spreadsheet. Remember:

- Total prize money uses the values: First prize, Second prize and Third prize
- Total income uses Number of competitors and Entry cost
- Money made uses Total income and Total prize money.

Activity 4.4

Write the expected result for each of the values that you wrote for **Activity 4.3**.

You will need to work out what the answer should be (use a calculator if you need to).

Activity 4.5

Enter the values in your spreadsheet. Note down whether you got the answer you were expecting.

If you did then that's great. If you didn't, then that also isn't a problem. This just means that you will have to look at the spreadsheet again and work out what went wrong. If you cannot work it out, ask your teacher to help you.

Activity 4.6

Create a second table. This time, change the values in the data input column.

- Work out the new results and write these in the table.
- Enter the new values in the spreadsheet. Did they work? Write down in your table whether they worked or not.

Skill 5

Modelling

When you have the formulas in your spreadsheet, you can change some of the data (the numbers that have been entered) and look at what else changes. This is called modelling.

Let's look at the Games Console spreadsheet.

Modelling 1: Changing data and watching what happens

What would happen if you didn't spend any money each week and saved all of your pocket money?

To test this, you need to change the data in Money spent each week to 0. Then look at whether the number of weeks changes.

Before:

Money spent each week = $3.50

Number of weeks = 123

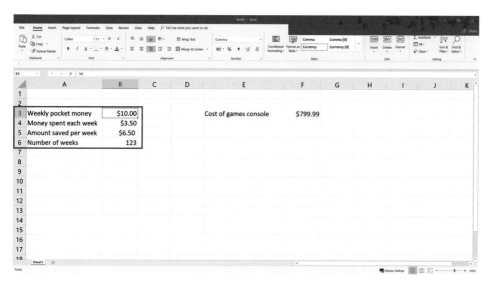

After:

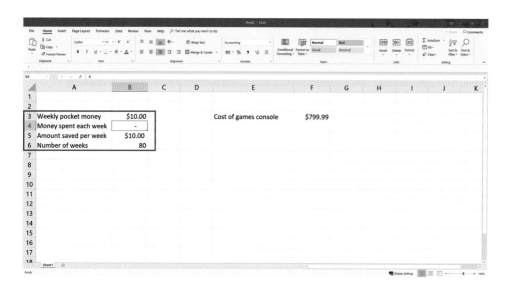

Money spent each week = $0 (-)

Number of weeks = 80

You can see here that by not spending that $3.50 a week, you could get the games console 43 weeks earlier!

Modelling 2: Changing data to get to an answer

You can also use modelling to try out different data until you get the answer that you want. For example, imagine that you want to buy the games console in 50 weeks. How much money would you need to receive in weekly pocket money to achieve this?

To answer this question, you will need to keep on changing the amount of weekly pocket money that you receive, until the number of weeks reaches 50.

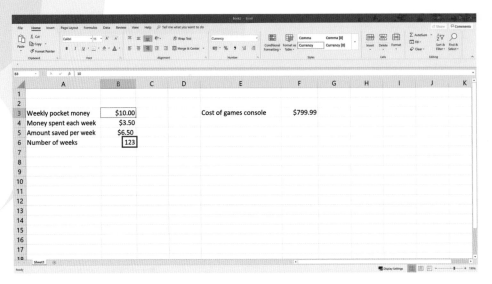

At the moment, the spreadsheet states 123 weeks. Now imagine that you need to make that number lower. To do this, you will need to increase the amount of weekly pocket money.

This time, try entering $20 and see what happens.

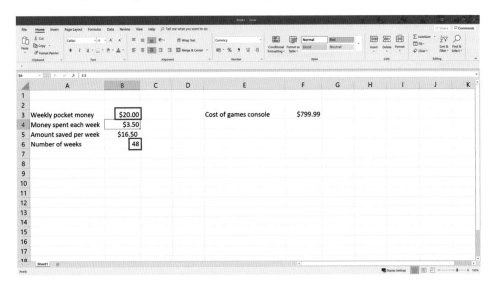

It is now listed as 48 weeks. That is very close, but it is less than 50.

This time, decrease the amount of money received and see what happens. Avoid making a big change here.

This time, try entering $19 and see what happens.

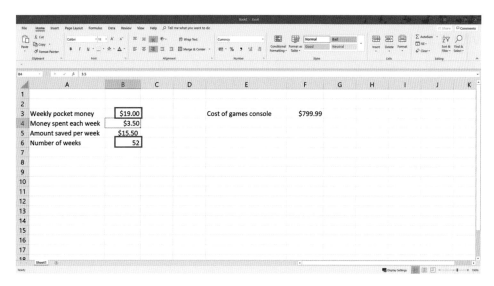

Now it is 52 weeks! You could change it again and try to make the number even closer. Why not try $19.5?

It now says 50 weeks. We got there!

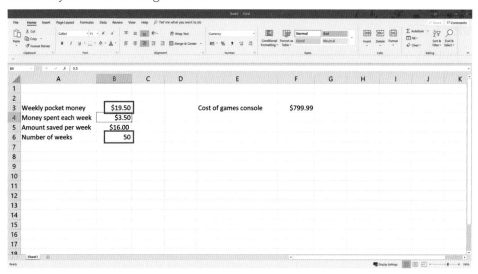

In conclusion, to buy this games console in 50 weeks, you would need to receive $19.50 a week in pocket money.

Activity 5.1

A new games console has been released that costs $999.99. Without changing the amount of money that you receive each week and the amount you save, find out how many weeks it will take for you to save for this new games console?

Activity 5.2

Now imagine you get a raise in the amount that you receive as your weekly pocket money. Add another $10 a week to the amount you currently receive. How many weeks will it take for you to save for the games console now?

Tip

For Activity 5.3, set the amount spent each week to 0, then change the amount of pocket money you receive.

Tip

Set the number of competitors to 280. Change the Price for entry until the Money made is as close to $2000 as you can make it.

Tip

Change the number of competitors to 200. You want Money made to be as near to $0 as possible but it cannot be below $0.

Tip

For **Activity 5.6**, set the number of competitors and price for entry. Change the first prize value until the Money made is as close to $0 as possible, but not below $0.

Activity 5.3

Now, you need to buy the games console in 90 weeks. If you didn't spend any money each week, how much weekly pocket money would you need to get to buy the console in 90 weeks?

Activity 5.4

Open your Ultimate League spreadsheet.

The organisers would like to make a profit (money made) of at least $2000. If there are 280 competitors, how much do they have to charge for entry to make $2000 profit?

Activity 5.5

The organisers of Ultimate League think that there are only going to be 200 competitors this year. What is the smallest amount that they can charge each competitor for entry, to make sure they do not make a loss?

Activity 5.6

The organisers of Ultimate League estimate that there will be 300 competitors and would like to charge them $5 each for entry. To be able to afford this, they would like to reduce the amount given for first prize. What is the highest first prize amount that they can set, without losing any money?

Skill 6

Create a data collection form

You will need to enter data into your database. Before you can do this you need to collect the data. You can do this using a form that you can create using a word processor, or by creating one on paper.

The data collection form needs to have:

- A suitable title (e.g. what the data collection is collecting data about)
- The name of each piece of data that someone needs to enter
- Space for people to write their answers
- All the possible options if there are only limited choices.

You will need several copies of this form, one for each item you are going to store. For example, in an online shop, each item of stock will be written on its own form. In a library, each book will be written on its own form.

To create a new data collection form, you will need to follow these steps:

1 Open a new document in Microsoft Word.
2 Save your document with a suitable name such as Book form.

3 Put a title in the top of the page. You can change the format, for example make it bold and centre aligned. Make sure any formatting you use is appropriate. The content is more important than it having lots of colours.

e.g.

Book Data Collection Form

4 If someone else will be filling in the form, write a (brief) introduction to tell them what to do.

e.g.

Please complete this form for one of your books. Write the information in the spaces provided.

5 Write your first field name. Next to it you need a space for the answer. This could be a box, or dots.

e.g.

Book Title [   ]

or

Book Title: ……………………………………………………………………………………..

6 Write your second field on the next line (you might want to leave an extra line of space for people who have large handwriting).

7 Continue until you have all your fields.

Special fields

1 If you have a field with options, you can ask them to choose one:

e.g.

Book genre (circle): Drama / Thriller / Crime / Action / Comedy / Other

2 If you have a field that needs specific data, e.g. a date or a 10-digit number, then you can show these spaces or structure using lines.

e.g.

Date of birth: …… …… / …… …… / …… ……

ISBN: …… …… …… …… …… …… …… …… …… …… …… …… …… ……

Now people know what the data should look like, and they can write one digit in each space.

When you have all the data on your form you need to test it. Print one copy of the form and write some example (real) data in it. Ask yourself these questions:

- Was there enough space?
- Was there anything missing?
- Was it easy to use? Do you need to add some instructions on what to do?

If you need to change your form you can. Make the changes, then test it again. Print a new copy and test it. You can repeat this as many times as you need to – it's important that your form is correct.

> **Tip**
>
> You can add images to your form if you want to enhance the presentation. Just make sure they are appropriate and relevant – they should not take over the page, the data is more important.

Here is an example form:

Books

Please complete this form for one of your books. Write the information in the spaces provided.

Book Title: ....

....

Author: ....

ISBN: ....

Genre (circle): Drama / Thriller / Crime / Action / Comedy / Other

Cost: $...... ....

Date of publication: .... / .... / ....

When you are happy with your form you can print as many copies as you need to fill in.

Skill 7

Formatting your spreadsheet

You can change the appearance of your spreadsheet to make it even more 'fit for purpose' (meaning more suitable for your audience). This can help make it easier to read by drawing attention to the key points.

Merge & Center
This combines several cells into one cell.

Key term

Merge & Center: make more than one cell become one cell.

Highlighting cells A1 to F2, then clicking on the **Merge & Center** button will make these cells into one cell.

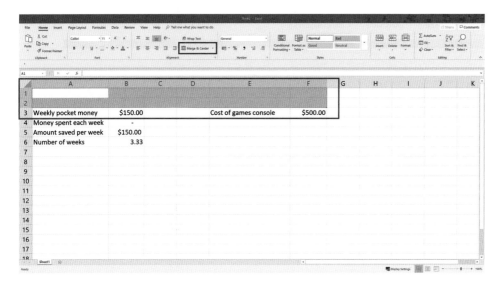

You can now put a title in this box.

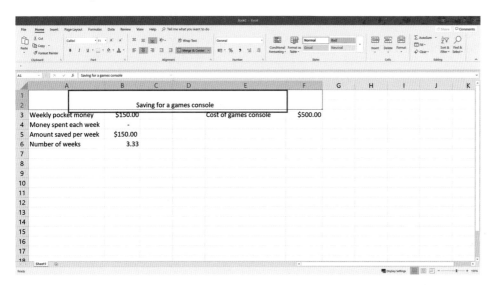

Formatting the font

When you click once on a cell, this enables you to change things like the font style and size.

You can make the font bold, italic and underlined. You can also change the colour and align your text to the left, the centre or the right.

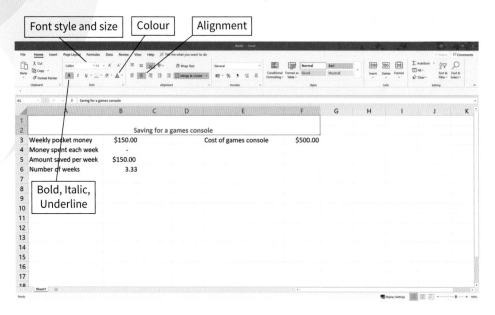

Cell colour

Click once on the cell if you want to change the colour.

Click on the arrow beside the fill bucket.

Then select a colour.

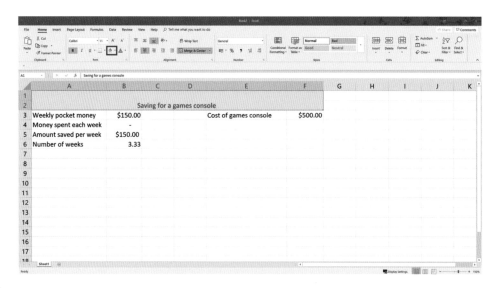

Cell border

You can add a border to an individual or group of cells.

Choose one border, or All Borders, to put lines around every individual cell.

You can also change the border colour (Line Color) and border style (Line Style).

These options will give you a pen icon. You will need to left-click on the edges that you would like to draw lines on.

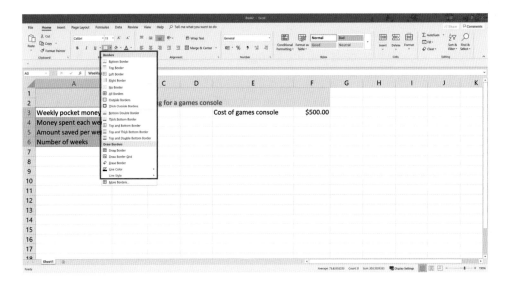

Activity 7.1

Add an appropriate title to your Ultimate League spreadsheet.

Make sure your title is:

- a larger font size than the rest of the font
- in bold
- centred over a number of cells. You will have to merge these cells.

Activity 7.2

Change the font style for the rest of the labels and data into your Ultimate League spreadsheet.

Make sure you use styles that are appropriate for your spreadsheet. Keep to a consistent theme and avoid using a different font style, size and colour for each cell.

Activity 7.3

Add borders to the cells that have labels and data in for your Ultimate League spreadsheet.

Make sure these borders are appropriate for your spreadsheet.

Make the border around the final profit value data larger and bolder than the others.

Activity 7.4

Change the background colour of some of the cells in your Ultimate League spreadsheet.

Think carefully about which cells you are going to choose to colour and which colour or colours you will use.

Make sure that the font is still visible over the colour. For example, avoid putting a dark blue font over a dark blue background.

Skill 8

Evaluating your spreadsheet

It is important to **evaluate** your work when you have finished. You will need to think about how well your spreadsheet works and if there is anything else you could do to improve it. You could, for example, ask yourself:

- Is your spreadsheet easy to use?
- Could you change anything to make the layout better?
- Is there anything within the spreadsheet that doesn't work?
- Would adding more formatting make it easier to use?
- Are there any other helpful features you could add? For example, conditional formatting.

These are just a few examples to get you started.

It is fine to say you do not think it works very well or if you have a list of things you would like to change. It doesn't mean you have done a poor job. It simply means you are good at being self-critical.

Compare your spreadsheet to your original plan. Remember, you created a list of objectives at the beginning of the chapter and now you need to check whether you have met those objectives.

First, create a table like this one. Put your objectives (from **Skill 1**, about the design) in Column 1. In Column 2, type in whether you have managed to achieve those objectives (meaning does your spreadsheet do the things you have asked it to).

Objective	Have I met the objective?
Record how much pocket money you get each week.	Yes, my spreadsheet lets me enter how much money I get each week. You can see this in cell B3.
Record how much extra money you have saved.	Yes, there is a cell that lets me enter my saved money total. This is in cell B4.
Record how much the games console will cost.	Yes, there is a cell available to record how much the games console will cost. This is in cell F3.
Work out how long it will take you to save enough money to buy the games console.	Yes. You can change the number of weeks in the spreadsheet and it will show you how much you will have saved. You can keep doing this until the number is the same, or more, than the cost of the games console.

Improvements

There is always something that you could do to improve your spreadsheet, even if you think it works well. Think about the following points:

- Is there anything in your spreadsheet that doesn't work? If so, then that problem needs fixing.
- Is your spreadsheet easy to use? Could the formatting be changed to make it even easier to use?
- Is there anything extra that you could add to make the spreadsheet better?
- Is there something you would do differently if you created the spreadsheet again?

You don't need to write pages of explanations. Just use short points. For example:

The spreadsheet doesn't look very interesting. I think it needs more formatting. The key data needs to be bolder in some way so that you can see the final answer straight away.

Activity 8.1

Create your own version of the objective table.

Type your objectives for the Ultimate League spreadsheet into the first column.

Type whether you have or haven't met each objective into the right-hand column.

For a more detailed evaluation, you can type into your objective table where the evidence can be found. For example, which cells to look at. This will make it easier for someone else to check your work and to make sure that you have met your objectives.

Activity 8.2

Write down three ways that you could improve your Ultimate League spreadsheet.

Think about the following:

- Is there anything that doesn't work?
- Could you make it easier to use?
- Could you add any additional features?
- Could it be created in a better way?

Skill 9

Presenting the results of a spreadsheet as a graph

Data within tables can be difficult to read and interpret. It is sometimes easier to view data in a graph. You can create graphs using a spreadsheet.

1 First, you need to highlight the columns that contain the data. Make sure that you also highlight the titles.

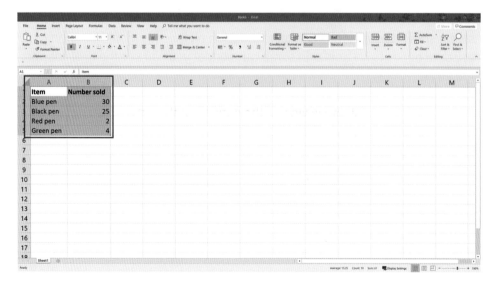

2 If the two columns are not next to each other, highlight one of them. Then hold down Ctrl on the keyboard and highlight the second one.

3 Click on the **Insert** tab from the menu.

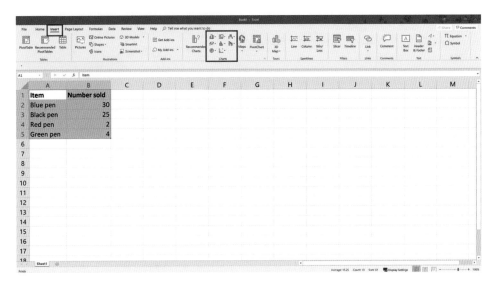

4 Choose one of the graphs from the options in the menu.

5 You can change the title of the graph by clicking on it. The title should describe what the graph shows.

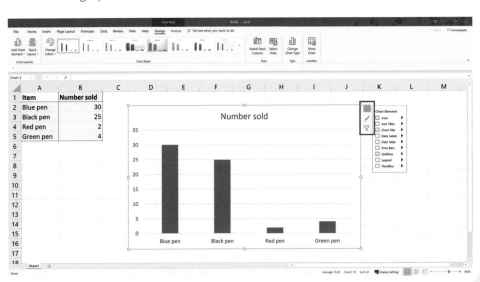

6 You can edit your graph by clicking on the options on the right-hand side:

- the + symbol lets you add axis titles.
- the paint brush symbol lets you edit the style of the graph.

You can change the format of just one part of a graph by clicking on it, then clicking on the **Format** tab on the menu. From here, you can change things like the fill colour and the outline.

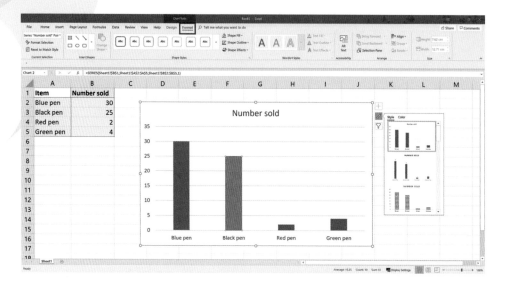

Activity 9.1

Open your Ultimate League spreadsheet.

1 In cell J1 enter the label: 'Number of competitors'.

2 In cell K1 enter the label: 'Money made'.

3 In cells J2 to J5, enter four different numbers of competitors, such as 250, 300, 350 and 400. Put one number in each row.

4 Enter the number of competitors into the spreadsheet model. Now enter the amount of money that each number of competitors made in column K.

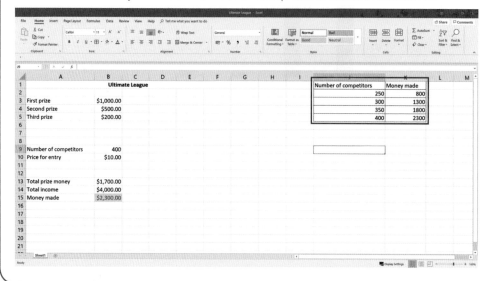

5 Create a line graph of this data to show how the amount of money made changes, depending on the number of competitors.

Make sure that you add an appropriate title and axis labels to the graph.

Activity 9.2

Open your Ultimate League spreadsheet.

Create a table to show the relationship between the first prize cost and the money made.

Create a line graph of this data to show how the amount of money made changes, depending on the first prize cost.

> **Tip**
>
> You will need to include a column with First prize cost and a column with Money made.

Scenario

Cake sale planning

Imagine that you are going to run a cake sale, to raise money for charity. You will bake cakes and then sell them to other students.

You need to work out how much it will cost you to bake each cake (your costs). Then you can work out how much to sell the cakes for (income). You want to try and make $100 profit.

The costs of ingredients are:

1000g flour = $0.78

200g butter = $0.99

1000g sugar = $1.88

1000g icing sugar = $2.20

12 eggs = $1.70.

20 cakes need:

200g flour

50g butter

200g sugar

200g icing sugar

2 eggs.

Tip

If one cake costs $0.10 to make and you sell it for $0.50, you will make $0.40 profit per cake. What information do you need to know, to work out these values?

Activity 1

1 Identify the objectives for the spreadsheet.

What inputs are required? What do you need to work out the cost of a cake and how much money you will make?

What information do you want from the spreadsheet? What are you trying to find out?

2 Identify the data you need to put into the spreadsheet.

Write a list of all the labels that you will need.

3 Identify the formulas that you will need to use within the spreadsheet.

Look at what you are trying to find out and how you are going to do this. Don't worry if you can't think of them all right now.

Activity 2

Create a new spreadsheet for the Cake Sale.

Add data labels for the data that you have identified in **Activity 1**.

Write in the data that you already know from the Cake Sale scenario.

Any data that you don't know, you can set to your own value, such as how much money you want to sell each cake for.

Activity 3

Add formulas to:

- work out the cost of one cake
- work out the profit for one cake
- work out how much money you will make if you sell a specific number of cakes, for example, 100.

Activity 4

Format your spreadsheet.

Add a suitable title. Add borders and appropriate background colours to the cells that you have used. Format the font appropriately as well.

Activity 5

Test your spreadsheet.

Create a testing table to test that your formulas work with the current data.

Complete the table by testing your spreadsheet.

Activity 6

Test whether your spreadsheet still works if you change data.

Create a testing table to test that your formulas still work.

Complete the table by testing your spreadsheet.

Activity 7

Use the spreadsheet to work out how many cakes you need to sell to make $100 profit.

Activity 8

Create a table and graph to show how the number of cakes sold affects the profit made.

Activity 9

Evaluate your spreadsheet by proving that it meets all of its objectives.

Compare your spreadsheet to each objective from **Activity 1**.

Activity 10

Write down the changes you had to make to your spreadsheet, as you created it.

Write down what your spreadsheet does well.

Write down how you could improve your spreadsheet.

Challenge 1

Conditional formatting

Conditional formatting changes the format of a cell, depending on what the cell has in it.

For example, you could turn the background of the cell green if the number in it is more than 0. You could also turn it red if the number is less than 0.

To change the background colour and/or the font style you need to:

1 Click on the cell that you want to format.

2 Click on the **Conditional Formatting** button (on the **Home** tab).

3 Click on 'Highlight Cell Rules'.

4 Choose your rule, such as 'Greater than', 'Less than', 'Equal to'.

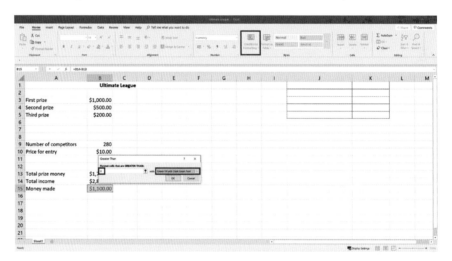

In this example, 'Greater than' has been chosen.

5 Enter the number in the first text box.

6 Either choose a pre-set format from the drop-down menu.

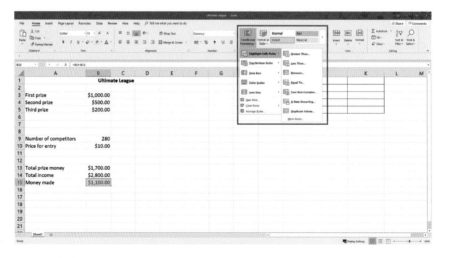

Or, click on 'Custom Format' and then choose your own options.

7 Click 'OK'.

Activity 1

Add conditional formatting to your Ultimate League spreadsheet.

When the money made is less than 0, turn the cell red.

Activity 2

When the money made is more than 0, turn the cell green.

Activity 3

When the money made is equal to 0, turn the cell orange.

Challenge 2

Goal seek

Microsoft Excel has 'What if?' functions built into it. Goal seek lets you tell the spreadsheet the value you are looking for. Then, it will change the values in your spreadsheet until it finds the value you want to use.

For example, if you want to find out how much you will need to charge to make $100 profit then it will change the entry fee until the profit is $100.

1 Click on the **What-If Analysis** button on the **Data** tab.

2 Click on 'Goal Seek'.

Key term

Goal seek: a tool that changes values for you, to reach the amount you want.

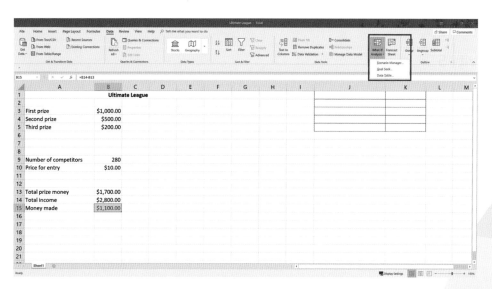

3 Click on the button to the right of 'Set cell'.

4 Click on the cell that you want to set a value to.
    You want the money made to be $2000 so click in B15, then click the 'Set cell' button again.

5   Type the value that you want to reach next to 'To value'.

6   Click on the button to the right of 'By changing cell'.

7   Click on the cell with the value that you want to change. You want to find out how much to charge, so click in B10, then click the 'By changing cell' button again.

8   Click 'OK' to see the result.

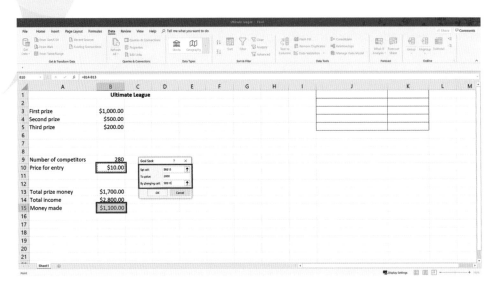

Activity 4

In your Ultimate League spreadsheet, use goal seek to find out how much you will need to charge for entry, if you want to make $2000 profit.

Activity 5

Use goal seek to find out how many people will need to enter for you to make $2000 profit, if you charge $20 for entry.

Activity 6

Use goal seek to find out how many competitors you will need to make $0 profit exactly, if you charge $10 entry per person.

Tip

You will need to enter the $20 entry fee.

Final project – holiday time!

You are thinking of going on holiday and need to work out which holiday you can afford and how long you can go for.

In your holiday group, there are two adults and four children who want to go on the holiday. You want to go for either 7, 10 or 14 days. You want all meals included in the holiday.

You have a maximum of $10 000 to spend.

There are three holiday choices.

Choice 1:	**Choice 2:**	**Choice 3:**
Sunset Resort.	Beach-view Point.	Crystal Sea Shore.
Adult: $430 for 7 nights	Adult: $80 for 1 night	Adult: $180 for 1 night
Child: $350 for 7 nights	Child: $70 for 1 night	Child: $140 for 1 night
All meals included	Adult meals: $30 for 1 day	Adult meals: $50 for 1 day
	Child meals: $25 for 1 day	Child meals: $30 for 1 day

Activity 1

Identify the objectives, data and formulas you will need to use in the spreadsheet.

Activity 2

Create a new spreadsheet and add the data labels that you will need.

Activity 3

Add the formulas into your spreadsheet.

Activity 4

Format your spreadsheet so it is appropriate for its intended use. Include conditional formatting to show whether you can afford the holiday or not.

Activity 5

Use goal seek to find out exactly how many days you could stay in a hotel without spending more than $10 000.

Activity 6

Test whether your spreadsheet works. Make sure you test the current data and also what happens if you change the data.

Activity 7

Evaluate your spreadsheet. Make sure you check whether it meets the objectives and that you discuss what your spreadsheet does well and how you could improve it.

Reflection

1 Why is using a computer model to try different values better than trying to work them out in real life?

_____

_____

_____

_____

_____

2 Why do you need to test your spreadsheet when you have finished creating it?

_____

_____

_____

_____

_____

_____

3 Why is it important to check that your spreadsheet meets its objectives?

_____

_____

_____

_____

_____

_____

4 Why does it not matter too much if your spreadsheet doesn't work first time?

_____

_____

_____

_____

_____

_____

Databases for a purpose

	In this module, you will learn how to:	Pass/Merit	Done?
1	Identify a purpose for a database	P	
2	Design, create and develop a database for a specific purpose	P	
3	Choose different data types	P	
4	Test your database	M	
5	Demonstrate an awareness of data security in a database	M	
6	Transfer data between different pieces of software.	M	

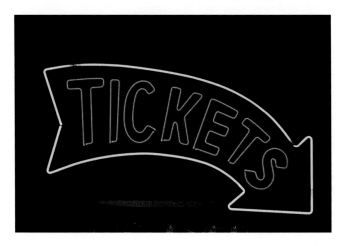

Did you know?

Databases are not only present on computers. They relate to any type of data storage. Paper files in a filing cabinet are still collectively known as a database.

In this module, you are going to develop new skills to help you work towards your final project. The final project will be to create a database used to store data relating to a school play. You will be in charge of ticket sales for the play and the whole school has asked you to create a database to store the information about the ticket sales.

You will also learn:

- how to edit a form
- how to add validation rules to a database
- how to create a query for your own database.

Before you start

You should:

- know what a database is and why it is used to store data
- be able to navigate a database
- be able to enter data into a database
- be able to choose and enter search criteria to create a query.

Introduction

Databases are used to store data in a structured, organised way. Having all the data in one place allows you to **interrogate** it, in order to find out useful information.

Databases are made up of one or more **tables**. A simple database has only one table, that is also known as a **flat file database**. It is not always the most efficient structure, but it is the easiest to create and set up.

Some databases that you may access in your day-to-day life are known as **distributed databases**. This means that the data is not always stored in one place. The data might be stored on lots of different computers. This means that when you search for something, it has to look for the search item across all of the places where it might be stored.

Skill 1	P

Identifying a purpose for a database

Databases are used by lots of people and organisations. This could be one person storing details of their DVD collection, or small organisations with a few employees, to large organisations with thousands of employees.

Databases are also used to store information that people need to access. This information can include:

- images
- videos
- books
- articles
- sound files.

An online music streaming service (such as Spotify) will have a database of all the music you can listen to. When you want to listen to one artist, you type in their name and the database **returns** all the songs they have. If you sign in to an account to listen to the music, then where do you think your username, password and other details are stored? In a database!

Key terms

Interrogate: to obtain data for a specific purpose.

Table: a structure with columns and rows, used for storing data in an organised way.

Flat file database: a database that has only one table.

Distributed database: a database where the data is split over several computers, not just stored in one place.

Stay safe!

Information is valuable. Be careful who you give your information to because it could be stored in a database for other people to access.

Find out what Data Protection legislation is, and how it protects you and your personal information.

Key term

Returns: a query finds data and gives you the values that meet the criteria.

An online shop will have a database with all the items that they have in stock. They will also have a database with all their customer details in, so next time you shop with them, you won't need to re-enter your name and address.

It is a good idea to try some activities relating to databases and their purposes.

Activity 1.1

Flying High Sports Club

You want to join the Flying High Sports Club and know that it stores information about its members in a database.

What is the purpose of this database?

Think about what information the club needs to collect from you and what they will use it for. Here are some of the reasons, given in the table.

Information	Example use
Name	So the club knows you are a member
	To give you a membership card
Address	So the club can post you letters
Email address	So the club can email you notices
Payment details	To allow the club to charge a monthly fee to you

What other information might the Flying High Sports Club collect from their members?

_____

_____

What could this information be used for?

_____

_____

Activity 1.2

An online shop will have one or more databases. What information will the shop store?

_____

_____

What could this information be used for?

_____

_____

Activity 1.3

A hospital will have one or more databases.

What information will the database(s) store?

_____

_____

Who will the information be about?

_____

_____

What can this information be used for?

_____

_____

Why might they need this information?

_____

_____

_____

_____

Activity 1.4

An organisation runs a computer game competition called Ultimate League. People pay to enter the competition and then take part in a number of games over a six-month period. The more games they win, the more points they get. At the end of each game, the player with the most points wins.

What information will the database(s) be storing?

_____

_____

Who will the information be about?

_____

_____

What will the information be used for?

_____

_____

Why does the organisation need this information?

_____

_____

Skill 2

Identifying fields for a database

Before you create a database, you need to decide:

- the purpose of the database
- the information that you need to collect, in order to fulfil that purpose
- the **fields** you are going to use.

A field is one, individual piece of data. This could be:

- your first name
- your last name
- your date of birth.

Data, such as your address, can be split into several fields. This will allow someone to use them on their own or together, so that there is a choice. You can include fields for:

- your house number or name
- your road name
- your town/city
- your country
- your postcode or zip code.

These are all entered individually, but they can be combined if you need them to be. For example, the database might let you search for all people who live in the country 'France' because the country where people live is an individual field.

To identify the fields that you want to use, you need to think about what information will be needed. For example, do you need to know where people live? It is important you only store information that you might need, otherwise you could be breaking **data protection regulations**.

Field names are usually short and meaningful. They say what they are storing. For example, 'Date of birth' is a better field name than 'The day, month and year that this person was born on'.

> **Key term**
>
> **Field:** one piece of data, such as a first name, or date of birth.

> **Stay safe!**
>
> Your data is valuable and should be kept private and secure. Remember to treat other people's data in the same way. Do not share the data you collect about people.

> **Key term**
>
> **Data protection regulations:** one or more laws that say what people can and can't do with other people's personal data.

Activity 2.1

Look back at the work you did in **Activity 1.1** in **Skill 1**. The Flying High Sports Club needs to store information about its members. The club needs to:

- be able to contact their members (by phone, email and letter)
- know which membership level they have chosen (bronze, silver, gold)
- be able to take a monthly payment from each member.

Write down a list of the field names that you might use for this database.

_____

_____

_____

_____

Activity 2.2

Look again at **Activity 1.4** in **Skill 1**. The creators of Ultimate League now want to collect some data about the people who have chosen to enter the competition. Each person in the competition can choose a game name. There are three age groups that they can enter: 8–12, 13–17, 18+. The creators will need to keep track of how many games each person has played and how many points they have gained.

Write down a list of the field names that you might use for this database.

_____

_____

_____

_____

Skill 3

Data types

When you store data in a computer, you will need to tell the computer what type of data it is. For example, it could be letters or numbers.

The table here describes some common **data types** that you might find in a database.

Data type	Description	Examples
Text	This will store combinations of letters (a–z, A–Z), symbols (e.g. !,./") and numbers, that you will not be doing calculations with (e.g. a telephone number).	New York Ouch! 1 is the first number 07784 999999
Number	This will only store numbers.	1 22 3.5 999.211
Date	This will store dates, i.e. day, month, year (you can change the order you want the date to be displayed in).	01/01/2000 09/10/2018
Boolean (e.g. Yes or No)	This will only store Yes or No.	Yes No
Currency	This will store numbers with a currency symbol, for example, $, £, €.	£100.99 $22.50

> **Key term**
>
> **Data type / field type:** a description of the type of data that will be stored: for example, letters or numbers.

Activity 3.1

Write the most suitable data type for each field, into the table.

Field name	Example data	Data type
First name	Frank, Linda, Khalid, Basma	
Temperature	22.2, 13.6, 28.5	
Date of birth	01/02/1977, 5/5/1998	
Salary	$12 000, £26 520	
Paid?	Yes, No	
Number of points	1, 10, 22	

Activity 3.2

Look at the fields that you have identified for the Flying High Sports Club in **Activity 2.1**.

Next to each field, write the most suitable data type.

Activity 3.3

Look at the fields that you have identified for Ultimate League in **Activity 2.2**. Next to each field, write the most suitable data type.

Skill 4

Creating a database table

Microsoft Access is a piece of software that allows you to create tables and produce queries to find information. You will be using Microsoft Access to create a database.

A table stores all the data about one 'thing'. The first row has the field names, then the data is underneath.

To create a new database you need to:

1   Open Microsoft Access.
2   Click on 'Blank database'.
3   Give the file a new, sensible name.

To create a new table:

1   Click on the **Create** tab.
2   Click on the **Table Design** button.

3   You then need to enter the field names into the first column.

4   Each field name goes on a new row.

5   Choose the data type in the second column. After this, click on the arrow to choose from the drop-down list.

> **Tip**
>
> When you try and save the table (click **File** then 'Save'), it might ask if you want to declare a Primary Key. Select 'No'.

Activity 4.1

Create a new database named 'Ultimate League'.

Create a new table named 'Players'.

Activity 4.2

Add the fields you identified in **Activity 2.2**.

Add the data type you chose in **Activity 3.3**.

Check your spellings carefully.

Skill 5

Creating a drop-down box

A **drop-down box** allows you to choose from set options.

It is used so you do not need to enter in your own text. It also means that the spellings will appear correctly (which is very useful when performing searches).

To set up a new drop-down box, you should:

1   Click on the data type for the field that you want a drop-down box to be placed on.

2   Choose 'Lookup Wizard'.

> **Key term**
>
> **Drop-down box:** a tool that gives the user options to choose from.

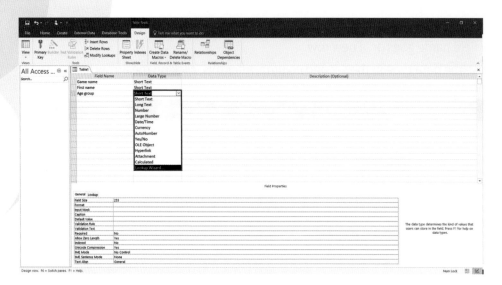

3 Click the circle next to 'I will type in the values that I want'.

4 Click on 'Next'.

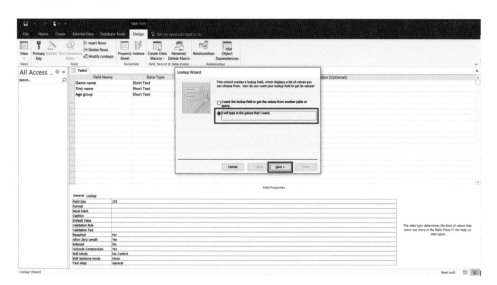

5 Type in each value on a new line. Make sure your spellings are correct.

6 Click 'Finish'.

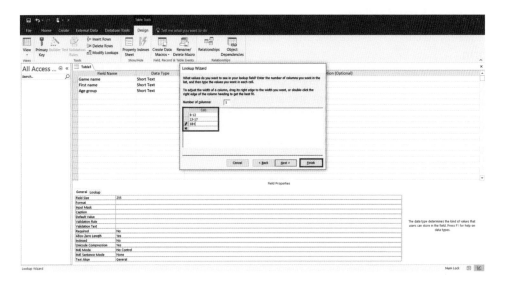

Activity 5.1

If you do not have a field to store the Ultimate League age groups, then add one. Create a drop-down box with the three age groups:

- 8–12
- 13–17
- 18+

Activity 5.2

The creators of Ultimate League would like to know the favourite type of games for all the people who have entered the competition.

Create a field to store this information and add a drop-down box with these options:

- racing
- adventure
- puzzle
- action
- combat
- other.

Think of some additional types of games and type them into the drop-down box.

Create a data entry form

In a database, you can enter data directly into the table or you can create a **data entry form**.

A form is a user-friendly tool that allows people to enter data. You can do things like change its appearance, change the font format and add buttons, to make it more appealing.

To create a new data entry form, you will need to follow these steps:

1 Open your database in Microsoft Access. You must already have your table created, to make a form.

2 Click on the **Create** tab.

3 Click on the **Form Wizard** button.

4 Choose your table from the drop-down list.

5 Click on the double arrow. This selects all fields. The fields will all move to the right-hand side.

6 Click on 'Next'.

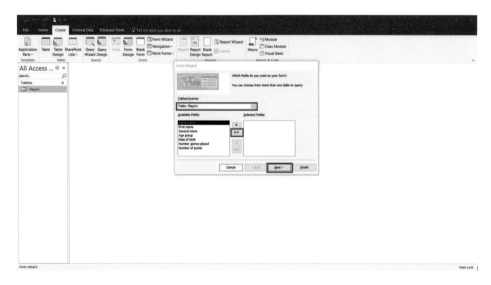

7 Click on 'Next' on the next screen ('Columnar' should be selected).

8 Give the form a suitable name.

9 Click 'Finish'.

Your form will open on-screen. You can now edit the form. (Go to **Activity 2** in the **Challenge** section to see how to do this.)

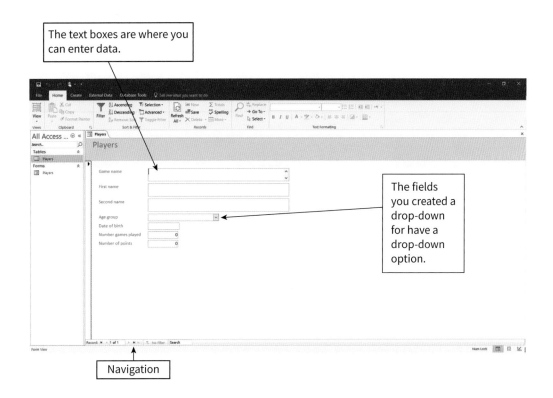

The text boxes are where you can enter data.

The fields you created a drop-down for have a drop-down option.

Navigation

Navigation buttons allow you to move between records and create a new record.

If you want to add a record to the database, don't change the text already in the text boxes.

Click on the **Create a new record** button. This gives you a blank form. Now you can enter your data.

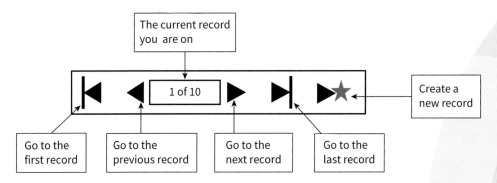

The current record you are on

1 of 10

Create a new record

Go to the first record

Go to the previous record

Go to the next record

Go to the last record

Activity 6.1

Create a data entry form for your Ultimate League Players table. Make sure you give it a sensible name, such as 'Players'.

Activity 6.2

1 Add a new player by filling in the empty form.
2 Click on the **New Record** button to get a new form.
3 Add another player.

Repeat these steps until you have entered ten players.

Skill 7

Testing your database

Whenever you create an application, you need to **test** that it works. If you don't test it properly, then you might not get the data you want.

Imagine if a hospital database was never tested and something went wrong. People's lives could be at risk!

When testing a database, you are going to need to take the following steps:

1 You need to decide what you need to test.
2 You need to state how you are going to test each point.
3 Once you have decided what to test and how to test each point, state whether the tests were correct and whether they worked.

Activity 7.1

You first need to test that your database includes all the fields you need.

Look at this description of the Ultimate League database:

An organisation runs a computer game competition called Ultimate League. People pay to enter the competition and then take part in a number of games over a six-month period. The more games they win, the more points they get. At the end, the player with the most points wins. Players can enter one of three age groups. The creators of Ultimate League would like to know the favourite type of games of all the people who have entered the competition.

Now look at your database table. Check each sentence in the description of the Ultimate League database against your database table.

Is there anything missing from your database?

_____

Don't worry if there is, you can add another field.

Activity 7.2

You can test whether you used the correct data type for each field.

Enter some new data into the database. Make sure you enter the correct type of data for each field. For example, if it should be a number, enter a number. If it should be a date, enter a date. Try entering the wrong type of data; for example, type a name into a date or numeric field and see what happens.

Does your database allow you to enter the data correctly?

Activity 7.3

You can test whether the drop-down boxes all work and include the correct options by following these three steps.

1 Identify the field(s) that you need a drop-down box for. You should include a drop-down box for the age group entered.

2 Identify what the drop-down box should say. The age groups options were 8–12, 13–17 and 18+.

3 Click on the drop-down box in your database and check these options are there.

Activity 7.4

Test whether your Ultimate League database has a working drop-down box for the players' favourite types of games.

Activity 7.5

You can check your data entry form works correctly by following these two steps:

1 Open your data entry form. Select a new record. Enter details for a new player.

2 Close your database. Then reopen it. If the player that you have just entered is still there, then it has worked.

Activity 7.6

You can check you have entered the data into the database accurately. This is called data **verification**. It does not check that the data is correct but it does check that it matches what you are told to enter.

Compare the data that you have entered into the database with the original copy. You might have copied it from a piece of paper or you might even have the person who the data belongs to, with you. Have you entered the data accurately?

> **Key term**
>
> **Verification:** checking that data is the same as the original and that it has been entered accurately.

Data security

Key terms

Digital footprint: the data about you that is available online.

Hack: gaining illegal, unauthorised access to a computer system.

Data Protection Legislation: laws that protect your data.

Password: a set of characters that only you know, which gives you individual access to a system.

Data can be personal and it can also be valuable. People pay a lot of money for data about other people such as where they live, what they like to buy and what they enjoy doing. This data is called your digital footprint. Everything you do online might be saved by the websites that you visit.

Have you ever wondered why advertisements appear on screen for products that you have recently been looking at? How does the website know what you have been looking at? Your search history is stored in your computer and when you visit sites, these websites access this particular data to show you advertisements for items that you appear to be interested in. This is a positive use of a **digital footprint** (at least for the advertisers; you might get annoyed by the adverts though!).

A digital footprint can also be used in a negative way. What will happen if one of your friends posts an image of you online that you don't like? That image could appear online for the rest of your life and could be accessed by anyone who wants to find out more about you, such as a future employer. Think about celebrities. They have photographs of themselves added online all the time, without their permission. Is that fair? They need some photographs for publicity but do they also have a right to privacy?

Data can also be used by criminals. Information such as your name, date of birth and address can be used to set up fake accounts pretending to be you or to **hack** into your own accounts to take your money.

It is important that data is always kept secure. By keeping it secure, it is less likely (but not impossible) that it can be stolen.

If you are storing data about other people, then it is important to remember that there are laws that say what you can and cannot store. These laws are known as **Data Protection Legislation**. One rule might be that you cannot store data about other people that you do not need, or that you need to keep other people's data secure.

The table here details some ways of keeping data in a database secure.

Method	Description
Password	Only people who know the password can access the data. The more complex the password, the harder it is to guess. A good password is more than eight characters long, includes numbers, symbols, lower-case and upper-case letters. Do not use words that are easy to guess, such as your name.

Method	Description
Access rights	You can limit what specific people can do within a database: 'Read only': The people who are 'Read only' can only view the data. They cannot edit it or delete it. 'Read, write': The people who are 'Read, write' can view the data, and change the data.
Views	In a database, you can set it up so that certain individuals can only view certain specific data. For example, a receptionist at a sports club may be able to view names and addresses but not sensitive data like credit card details or a person's medical history.

You do not need to know how to set these options up within your database, but you need to know what they are, and why they are used.

Access rights and views are different. Some people can have 'read-only' access to a database, but will be able to view all of the data. A different person can have 'read, write access' to the database, but they can only 'view' a small part of the database.

Activity 8.1

The people running Ultimate League need to know how to keep the data in their database secure.

Using the information above, describe two ways that the creators of Ultimate League can keep their data secure.

1 _____

_____

_____

2 _____

_____

_____

Transferring data to a word processor

You might need to use the data in your database in a word-processed document, for example to write a letter to someone whose address is stored within the database.

You can transfer the data directly to that document, which is a faster and more accurate method than trying to type it all out again. You can do this by:

- **exporting** the data from the database
- **importing** the data into the word processor.

There are lots of different ways that you can export data from a database. For example, you can copy and paste data, or export it directly from Microsoft Access.

Another way would be to export it to another piece of software, such as Microsoft Word. The method that you choose depends on what you want the data to look like and how you want to use it.

Method 1: Copy and paste

This method will copy all the data that you have selected from the database table into your word processor document. This data will be copied in a table format.

To copy and paste the data you will need to follow these five steps:

1 Open the table.

2 Highlight the grey boxes on the left of the fields.

3 Click on the **Copy** button.

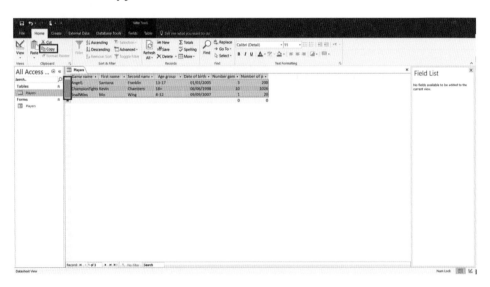

4 Open your word processor file.

Key terms

Export: to take data out of one piece of software.

Import: to put data into a piece of software.

Tip

This is the simplest method to use. The other methods are more advanced ways of doing this.

5 Click on the **Paste** button.

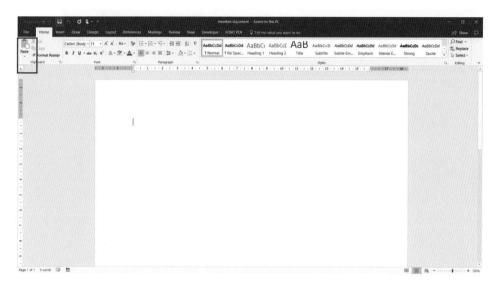

You can then edit your data as you need to.

Method 2: Access Export

This will create a new document with the data added to it, such as a Microsoft Word document.

You can export the data to create a new word-processed document.

To export the data, you will need to follow these seven steps:

1 Click on the **External Data** tab.

2 Click on the **More** button.

3 Click 'Word'.

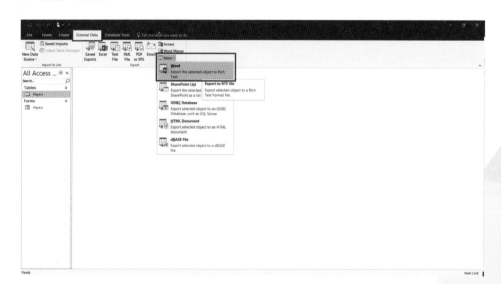

4 Click 'Browse'.

5 A new window will open. Choose the folder where you want to file to appear.

6 Click 'OK'.

7 In the next window, click 'Close'.

You will now have a new Microsoft Word file with the data from your table.

Tip

Mail merge is not on the syllabus, but it is an important use of data in databases.

Method 3: Mail merge

If you write a letter that needs to be sent to lots of different people, you will only want to include one person's name and address on each letter. If you use the copy and paste function, you will have to copy each person's details one at a time. For example, a school might need to send a letter to all the parents and guardians of the students, telling them about a school play. The school only wants one parent's or guardian's name and address detailed on each letter.

Mail merge will produce just one copy of your document for each record within your database. If each person has a new record, then there will be one document per person.

The information does not just have to be for a letter, it could be used to create a personalised badge, poster or certificate for each person that includes their name on it.

To create a mail merge you will need to follow these ten points:

1 Open your database in Microsoft Access.

2 Click on the **External Data** tab.

3 Click on the **Word Merge** button.

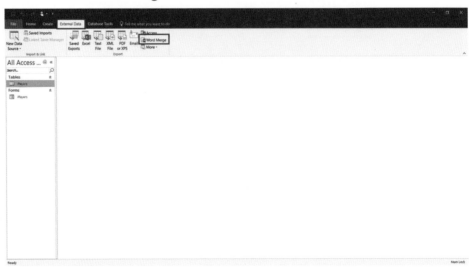

4 Click on 'Create a new document and then link the data to it'.

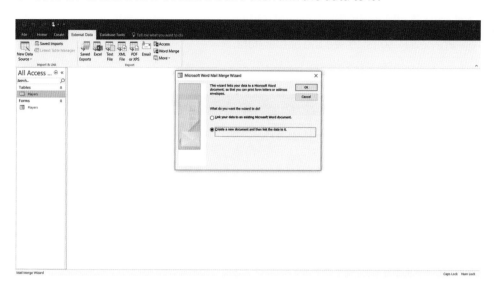

5 Click on 'OK'.

6 A new Microsoft Word document will open with a bar positioned on the right-hand side. You can close this bar by clicking on the cross.

7 Click on the **Insert Merge Field** button.

This will show all the fields in your database.

8 Click on the field you want in your Microsoft Word document.

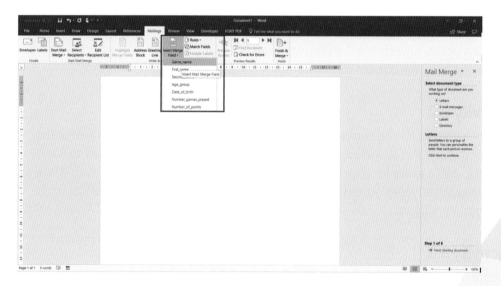

9 Select each field you would like to use individually.

They appear with << and >> around the field names.

10 Click on 'Preview Results' to see the actual data.

Use the arrows to move between each record.

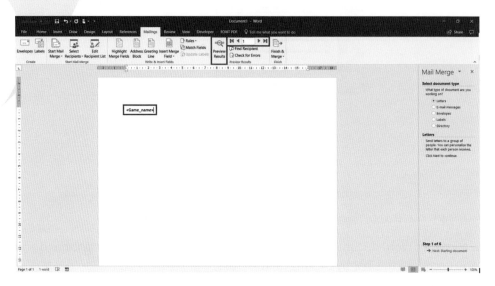

You can now format your document in the way that you want, such as adding text, to create your document.

Activity 9.1

Create a poster advertising the Ultimate League. Export the names of the games belonging to all the players in your database, onto the poster.

Activity 9.2

Create a register for the competitors to sign, to confirm that they have arrived at the competition. It should include the game name, first name and last name of all the players, with a space for them to sign their name to say that they have arrived. Make sure the register looks attractive. You could do this by including a suitable title and appropriate images.

Activity 9.3

Create a letter that tells each competitor the number of games that they have played and the number of points that they have gained. Address the letter to each individual, using just their first name and last name. Each player should receive their own letter with only their details on it.

Skill 10

Transferring data to a spreadsheet

You can transfer data from a database into a spreadsheet. A spreadsheet has a series of cells that can store data and can perform mathematical calculations using numeric data. A spreadsheet can be useful to organise data which you can then use to create graphs from the data.

Method 1: Copy and paste

1 Copy the data across in the same way as shown in **Skill 9 Method 1: Copy and paste**.

2 Open Microsoft Excel.

3 Click on the **Paste** button.

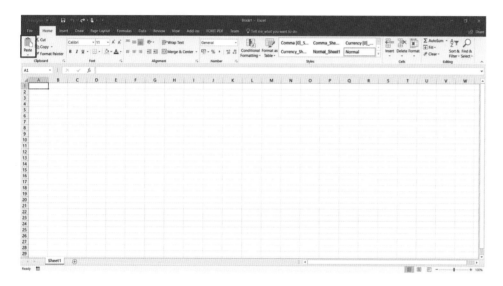

Method 2: Access Export

1 Open your Microsoft Access database.

2 Click on the **External Data** tab.

3 Click on the **Excel** button.

4 Click 'Browse', choose where you want to create the spreadsheet, then click 'Save'.

5 Click 'OK'.

6 On the next screen, click 'Close'.

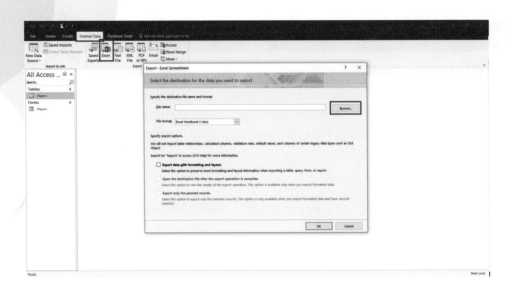

You will have a new spreadsheet in the folder that you exported it to.

Method 3: Spreadsheet Import

1 Open a new Microsoft Excel file.

2 Click on the **Data** tab.

3 Click on the **Get Data** button.

4 Click 'From Database'.

5 Click 'From Microsoft Access Database'.

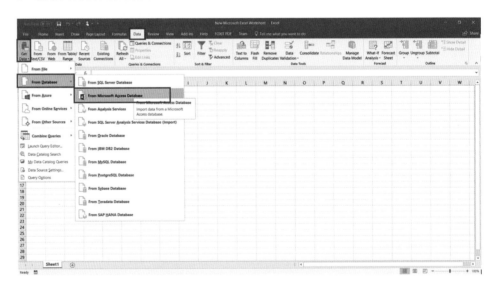

6 Find and select your database.

7 Select your database table.

8 Click 'Load'.

Activity 10.1

Create a spreadsheet containing all the data in your Ultimate League database.

Activity 10.2

Order the information on your spreadsheet to display the players in descending order of points earned (the player with the highest number of points is at the top).

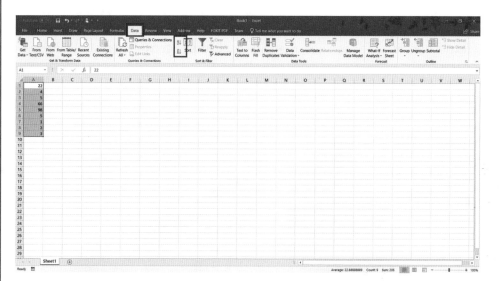

Tip

To order the data in a column, first click anywhere within the column. From the menu, choose **Data** and select either ascending, or descending order.

Activity 10.3

Create a graph detailing the number of games that each player has played. Use the player's game name as well as the number of games.

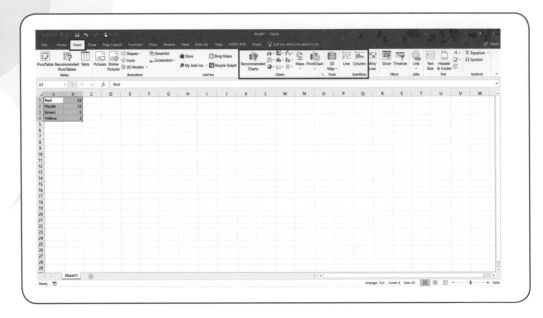

Scenario

School library

This school library needs a database to store information about the books that it has stored in the library.

Each book has a title and a main author. It also has an ISBN number and belongs to a particular type of genre (such as action, romance or crime). The library would also like to record additional details such as the year it was published, the number of pages it has and who the book is aimed at (such as adults, or children aged 0–5 years). They also want to keep track of how many times it has been loaned out.

Activity 1

Describe the type of database that the library needs.

Identify:

- the purpose of the database
- what the library will be able to use the database to do
- the people who will use the database
- what each person will use the database to do.

Activity 2

List the fields that need to be stored about each book.

Make sure you have chosen appropriate field names.

Activity 3

For each field that you identified in **Activity 2**, choose an appropriate data type for the data.

Activity 4

Create a new database and table for the library.

Create a drop-down box for at least one field in your table.

Activity 5

Create a user input form for your table.

Activity 6

Use your user input form to add at least ten books to your database.

Activity 7

Create a list in a word processor that includes the name, author and genre of all of the books in the library.

Activity 8

Create a graph, using a spreadsheet, of the name of each book and the number of times it has been loaned out by the students.

Activity 9

Write a report for the school librarian, telling them why it is important that the data is kept secure, and how they can keep the information in the database secure.

Activity 10

Describe three ways that you will test that your database works.

Challenge 1

Validation rules

Key term

Validation: checking that data is suitable.

You can put restrictions on data input into a database. This called **validation**. This can be used to stop people from entering inappropriate data, for example a name should not be "123456!".

If you include a drop-down box, you can stop anything else being input in the database.

1   Open the table in design view. Click on the **View** button and choose 'Design'.

2   Click on the field where you need to add the validation rule to.

3   In the box 'Validation Rule', type each option in speech marks (" ") with the word 'Or' in-between, for example "8–12" Or "13–17" Or "18+".

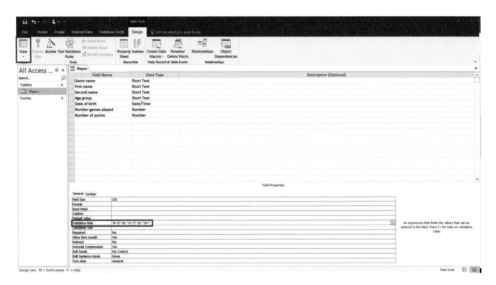

This means only 8–12, or 13–17, or 18+, can be entered. Anything else will create an error message.

You can write your own error message in the box 'Validation Text'.

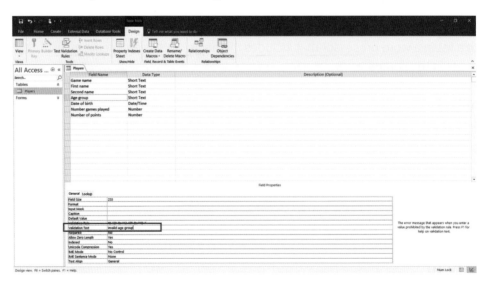

126

You can add numeric validation too, using these symbols:

- < less than
- <= less than or equal to
- > greater than
- >= greater than or equal to.

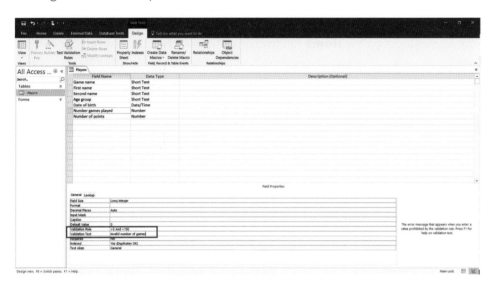

Use the key word 'And' to combine more than one option, for example >0 and <100 means the number entered must be more than 0 and less than 100.

Activity 1

Add a validation rule for the Age group in the Ultimate League.

Activity 2

Add a validation rule for Number of games played and Number of points in the Ultimate League database.

Challenge 2
Edit the design of a form

You can change the design of a form to make it more attractive and appropriate for the user and information that it contains.

1 Open the form in **Design View**. Click on the **View** tab, then 'Design'.
2 Click on a text box, or the background of part of the form, to change that area.
3 Use the format tools on the **Home** tab to change the font type and background colour.

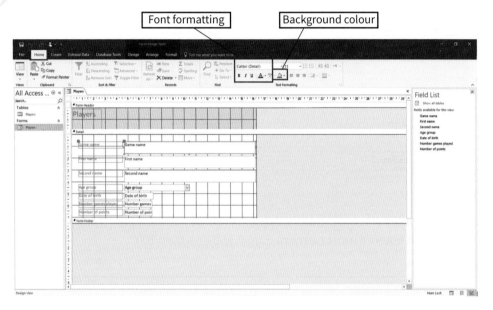

Font formatting

Background colour

4 Open the form in 'Data View'. Click on **View** and then **Data** to use the form again.

Activity 3

- Change the design of your user input form for the Ultimate League.
- Change the font style, size and colour.
- Change the background colour of the forms.

Challenge 3

Create a query

A **query** allows you to select only the specific information that you want to view or use. For example, you could search for all people under the age category 18+. This means that you do not have to search through data that you do not need.

Key term

Query: a tool that allows you to search for specific data.

To create a new query

1 Click on the **Create** tab.

2 Click on the **Query Design** button.

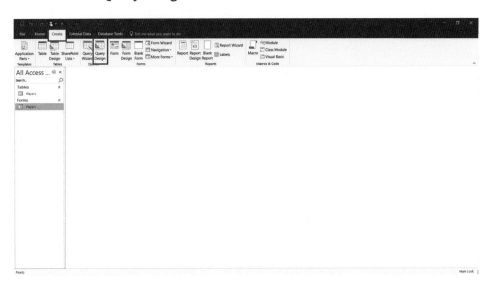

3 Click on the name of your table.

4 Click on 'Add'.

5 Click on 'Close'.

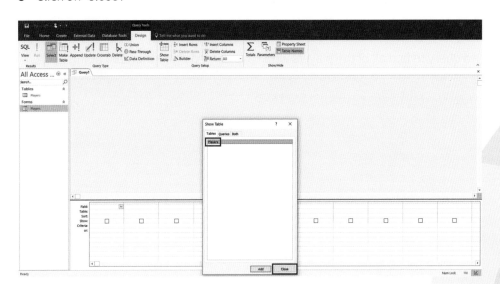

6 Double-click on each field you want to be displayed.

7 Enter the criteria for a field in the 'Criteria' row.

For example, the criteria here will only display records where the 'Age Group' is 18+.

If this is text, it needs to be put in speech marks such as "18+". Access will automatically add the speech marks for you.

8 Click on 'Run' to see the results.

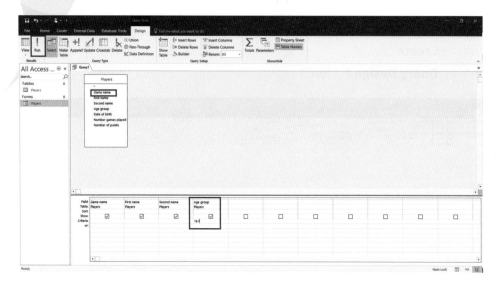

Tip

You won't need any criteria for this query.

Tip

Greater than 100 is written as >100.

Activity 4

Create a query to find the game name for all players in the competition.

Activity 5

Create a query to find all of the players in the age group that are aged 18+.

Activity 6

Create a query to find all of the players who have earned more than 100 points.

Challenge 4
Create a report

Data in a database can be turned into a document that you can then print or use elsewhere. The **report** format is more user-friendly than looking at a table.

1 Open your Microsoft Access database.

2 Click on **Create**.

3 Click on the **Report Wizard** button.

4 Click on the drop-down menu and choose the table, or query, where you want to take the data from.

> **Key term**
>
> **Report:** a tool that allows you to put data into a user-friendly format for printing.

5 Click on the fields that you would like to include within your report and click on the single arrow to move them to the right-hand side.

6 Click 'Finish'.

7 Click 'Close Print Preview' to edit your report.

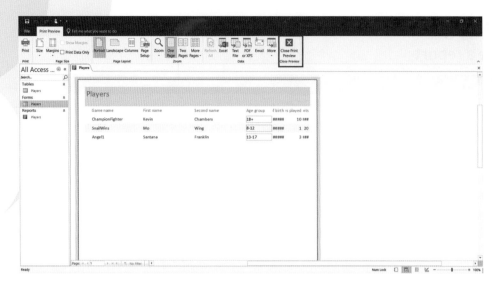

You can now move the text boxes and use the editing tools at the top of the screen to change your report.

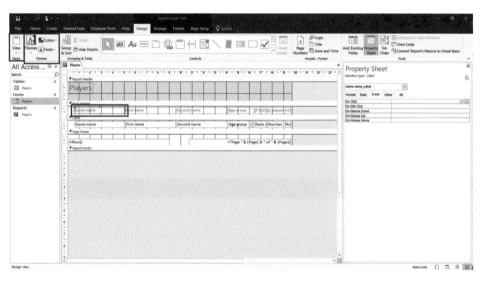

You can make the boxes wider by clicking on them and then dragging the yellow boxes so that they appear wider.

Click on the **View** button. 'Report' view lets you see the data. 'Design' view lets you edit your report.

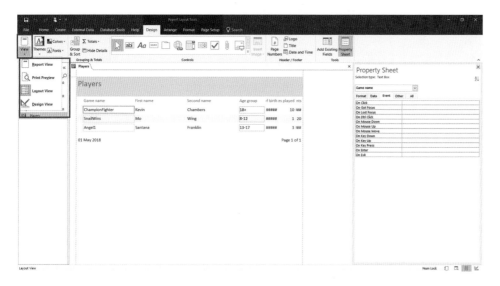

Final project – selling tickets for the school play

Your school is putting on a school play. They are selling tickets to parents, guardians, carers and friends of the students. The school needs a database to keep track of who has bought tickets. They will also need to post, or email, the tickets to the people who have bought them. Each individual person can buy a maximum of ten tickets.

Activity 1

Describe the database that the school needs.

Identify:

- the purpose of the database
- what the school will be able to use the database to do
- the people who will use the database
- what each person will use the database for.

Activity 2

Make a list of the fields that the database will require. Choose appropriate date types for the data. Create a new database and table, using the fields that you have identified.

Make sure that at least one field has a drop-down box.

Add at least one validation rule to your table.

Activity 3

Create a data entry form for the table that you have created. Use your form to add a minimum of ten ticket sales to your database.

Edit your data entry form to make it more appropriate.

Activity 4

Use a word processor to write a letter to the people who have bought tickets. Remind them of the time and date of the play, as well as the number of tickets that they have bought.

Activity 5

Write a report to the school telling them why it is important that the data is kept secure and how they can keep it secure. Merge the data from your database into your letter.

Activity 6

Write down three ways you could test that your database works.

Activity 7

Create a query to find all the people who have bought more than two tickets.

Reflection

1 How many databases do you usually access each day? Think about what you use computers for, such as the internet and so on. List the data that is stored in these locations.

_____

_____

_____

_____

_____

_____

2 Explain why it is important to keep data secure.

_____

_____

_____

_____

_____

_____

3 Explain why an electronic database is better than storing data on paper.

_____

_____

_____

_____

_____

_____

Acknowledgements

The authors and publishers acknowledge the following sources of copyright material and are grateful for the permissions granted. While every effort has been made, it has not always been possible to identify the sources of all the material used, or to trace all copyright holders. If any omissions are brought to our notice, we will be happy to include the appropriate acknowledgements on reprinting.

Thanks to Getty Images for permission to reproduce images:

Cover Julos/Getty Images

Inside kemie/GI; Alan Tunnicliffe Photography/GI; ZenShui/GI; alengo/GI; andresr/GI; skynesher/GI; kemie/GI; Hero Images/GI; C.Thatcher/GI; kali9/GI; THEGIFT777/GI; Imgorthand/GI; Peter Dazeley/GI; TheCrimsonMonkey/GI; Hero Images/GI; Alan Schein Photography/GI; Antonio_Diaz/GI; Panama7/GI; bubaone/GI; FangXiaNuo/GI; Jupiterimages/GI

Image for online activity Caiaimage/Robert Daly/GI.

Key: GI = Getty Images